T0306181

"There are many reasons to preserve our national parks: beauty, biodiversity, recreation, history, and patriotic pride. But an old adage says that whoever makes the economic argument first wins. Linda Bilmes and John Loomis give us one more reason national parks must be preserved, their extraordinary economic value."

—*Jonathan Jarvis, Director, National Park Service 2009–2017*

"Linda Bilmes, John Loomis and their collaborators have calculated a value of the priceless – our nation's natural, historic and cultural treasures cared for by the National Park Service. Their work makes an important case for supporting these irreplaceable assets not just for today, but to inspire generations to come."

—*Sally Jewell, U.S. Secretary of the Interior, 2013–2017*

"We live at a time when our most treasured conservation and wildlife resources are under relentless attack. We owe a debt of gratitude to Linda Bilmes and John Loomis, for their pioneering book that validates the real economic value and growth created by our National Parks. Every person who values these treasures needs to read this important mandate for change."

—*Tony Knowles, Governor of Alaska (1994–2002),*
Chair of the National Park System Advisory Board (2010–2018)

"Linda Bilmes and John Loomis provide an analysis of what millions of American park visitors know in their hearts: Our parks are a national treasure deserving strong public support."

—*Philip Sharp, Member of Congress (1975–1995);*
President, Resources for the Future (2005–2015)

"Ever since the great statistician and economist Harold Hotelling responded in 1949 to an inquiry from the Director of the National Park Service by outlining a methodology for carrying out monetary valuation of recreation in the National Parks, economists have diversified and improved methods for valuing this precious treasure – our system of National Parks. In this new volume, Linda Bilmes, John Loomis, and their co-authors offer a comprehensive picture of the value of U.S. National Parks, and thereby provide a compelling justification for sustainable funding for their preservation in perpetuity."

—*Robert N. Stavins, A.J. Meyer Professor of Energy and*
Economic Development, Harvard Kennedy School,
Cambridge, Massachusetts, USA

Valuing U.S. National Parks and Programs

This book provides the first comprehensive economic valuation of U.S. National Parks (including monuments, seashores, lakeshores, recreation areas, and historic sites) and National Park Service (NPS) programs.

The book develops a comprehensive framework to calculate the economic value of protected areas, with particular application to the U.S. National Park Service. The framework covers many benefits provided by NPS units and programs, including on-site visitation, carbon sequestration, and intellectual property such as in education curricula and filming of movies/TV shows, with case studies of each included. Examples are drawn from studies in Santa Monica Mountains National Recreation Area, Golden Gate National Recreation Area, Everglades National Park, and Chesapeake Bay. The editors conclude with a chapter on innovative approaches for sustainable funding of the NPS in its second century. The framework serves as a blueprint of methodologies for conservationists, government agencies, land trusts, economists, and others to value public lands, historical sites, and related programs, such as education. The methodologies are relevant to local and state parks, wildlife refuges, and protected areas in developed and developing countries as well as to national parks around the world.

Containing a series of unique case studies, this book will be of great interest to professionals and students in environmental economics, land management, and nature conservation, as well as the more general reader interested in National Parks.

Linda J. Bilmes is the Daniel Patrick Moynihan Senior Lecturer in Public Policy at the Harvard Kennedy School, Harvard University, U.S.A.

John B. Loomis is Professor in the Department of Agricultural and Resource Economics, Colorado State University, U.S.A.

Valuing U.S. National Parks and Programs

America's Best Investment

**Edited by Linda J. Bilmes and
John B. Loomis**

LONDON AND NEW YORK

First published 2020
by Routledge
2 Park Square, Milton Park, Abingdon, Oxon OX14 4RN

and by Routledge
52 Vanderbilt Avenue, New York, NY 10017

Routledge is an imprint of the Taylor & Francis Group, an informa business

British Library Cataloguing-in-Publication Data
A catalogue record for this book is available from the British Library

Library of Congress Cataloging-in-Publication Data
A catalog record has been requested for this book

ISBN: 978-1-138-48310-1 (hbk)
ISBN: 978-1-138-48312-5 (pbk)
ISBN: 978-1-351-05578-9 (ebk)

Typeset in Sabon
by Deanta Global Publishing Services, Chennai, India

Contents

Figures

Tables

Preface

The idea for this book originated in the work of the Second Century Commission, a bipartisan group of experts convened by the National Parks Conservation Association to explore how the National Park Service (NPS) should chart its path forward in its second century. Linda J. Bilmes, who served on the Commission, led a subcommittee that examined the current funding structure of the NPS. It concluded that annual congressional appropriations funding model was not sufficient to sustain the long-term mission of the NPS, and was contributing to a large and growing backlog of critical conservation and maintenance work.

In order to make the case for a more sustainable funding structure, NPS needed to demonstrate the significant economic value that it delivers to the American public. The NPS traditionally has measured this value primarily in terms of tourism at National Parks. While tourism is clearly important, it represents only one element of the overall benefit provided by the NPS.

This cause was embraced by the National Park Service Advisory Board, the congressionally mandated group of 12 individuals who advise the Director of the National Park Service and the Secretary of the Interior on matters related to the National Park system. Linda was one of several Board members who had previously served on the Second Century Commission and led the work in this area. John B. Loomis, an expert in economic valuation of non-marketed natural resources, was chosen to join Linda and other Board members in an effort to define and quantify the many other economic benefits that NPS provides.

This book is the first effort to derive a comprehensive estimate of those benefits. Our starting point was to map out the many sources of value of the National Parks and NPS programs. These included activities that are often overlooked, such as carbon sequestration, education and curriculum development, iconic movies filmed in the National Parks, and NPS cooperative programs with local governments and non-governmental organizations. We then launched an effort to document some of these major benefit areas, and to develop an analytical framework to quantify their economic value. This effort included the design and implementation of a major survey of the American public designed to reveal the 'hidden' value to individuals from many walks of life who derive direct or indirect benefits from the National Parks and their programs.

Although we were not able to quantify every benefit, the magnitude of the total economic value is quite startling. Using conservative methodology, the benefits add up to over $100 billion annually, of which more than one-third accrues to people who never set foot in the National Parks themselves. This figure throws new light on the significant value delivered by the NPS from its annual federal budget of just $2.5 billion. We believe it makes a powerful case for a reform of the NPS financing in order to fulfill its mission to protect the National Parks for current and future generations. A number of potential reforms to the funding model are examined in this book, that we believe would place the NPS on a more sustainable footing for the next century.

Together we have worked to investigate the economic contributions of National Parks Service. The culmination of this research endeavor is presented in this book.

Linda J. Bilmes and John B. Loomis

Acknowledgments

Many of our colleagues have given generously of their time to make this book possible. Above all, we benefitted from the wise counsel and encouragement of Jonathan Jarvis, who served as the 18th Director of the National Parks Service and Dr. Bruce Peacock, the agency's lead economist. We are also grateful for advice and support from Sally Jewell, Secretary of the U.S. Department of Interior from 2013 to 2017, who was a member of the original Second Century Commission, and to the wonderful members and staff of the National Parks Service Advisory Board, including Paul Bardacke, Leonore Blitz, Judy Burke, Milton Chen, Rita Colwell, Belinda Faustinos, Carolyn Finney, Loran Fraser, Gary Machlis, Tony Knowles, Gretchen Long, Stephen Pitti, Shirley Sears, and Margaret Wheatley.

We would in particular like to thank Linda's students who contributed to our research over many years. These include Adam Banasiak, Stephanie Bailenson, Francis Choi, Tyler Evilsizer, Thomas Liu, Timothy Marlowe, Michael Silah, and Stephen Thompson. Several of them have co-authored chapters of this volume.

We also thank Linda's colleagues at Harvard who helped us throughout, especially Henry Lee, Dutch Leonard, Scott Leland, James Levitt, and Yahya Chaudhry and the Directors of the Harvard Environmental Economics Program, Robert Stavins (who first introduced us) and Robert Stowe.

We also wish to thank David Golden, who kindly loaned us the beautiful conference room at Revolution Ventures in San Francisco to write the sustainable funding chapter.

We are especially grateful for the funding for this research, which has been provided by Tina Batt, of the S. D. Bechtel, Jr. Foundation, Mike Finley of the Turner Foundation, Cody J. Smith of the Summit Foundation, Will Shafroth of the National Park Foundation and Bryan Richardson of UPD Consulting.

We also thank a number of people who have advised us on portions of the research that we drew on for this book. They include Milton Chen, Sylvia Earle, Henry Louis Gates, Jr., Belinda Faustinos, James Levitt, Gretchen Long, and Colin Mayer.

This book and several of its chapters benefitted from the input and assistance of a number of individuals in the NPS, including Dr. Bruce Peacock, Dr. Lynne Koontz, Dr. Leslie Richardson, and Julia Washburn.

John B. Loomis thanks Dr. Sandra Gudmundsen (Chapters 1, 2 and 9) and Dr. Michelle Haefele (Chapter 4) for their numerous editorial suggestions that have clarified the text of several chapters, and thereby spared readers of this book from significant confusion at times. Linda J. Bilmes thanks Ken Norris and Yahya Chaudhry for assistance with Chapter 6 and Chapter 7, respectively.

We both thank the extraordinary men and women who work for the NPS and contribute their lives to sustaining this national treasure.

Finally, we thank our families for their love and support throughout this process.

Of course, none of these funding groups or individuals are responsible for the contents of this book or its conclusions, which are solely those of the authors.

Valuing U.S. National Parks and Programs: America's Best Investment
Foreword

Catherine Kling

Economists have studied the value of individual protected areas such as National Parks for decades, but they have rarely tackled the valuation of an entire system of National Parks or protected areas. Further, most of these past efforts have focused on recreation use values and associated tourism of National Parks, potentially ignoring substantial values to those who do not directly consume these unique public lands.

Since the mid-1960s when John Krutilla published his famous article in *American Economic Review*, economists have recognized that benefits accrue to people who do not visit or otherwise directly 'consume' National Parks. Economists have categorized these values as non-use values: benefits from knowing these areas exist, and benefits from knowing protection today will provide these areas to future generations. These non-use values have been measured at a few National Parks in the USA and wilderness areas around the world.

For the first time, the research in this book takes the final step. The authors provide the first encompassing estimates of the use and non-use values for the *entire* National Park system in the USA. These values include not just the values of the grand natural wonders of National Parks that immediately come to mind (e.g., the Yosemite, Yellowstone, Grand Canyon), but also the important but often overlooked historic sites that are protected by the National Park Service (NPS). In addition, the book values the dozens of NPS programs that provide benefits from aiding communities to protect natural and historic resources located outside of National Parks.

Many of us have suspected that the National Parks and NPS programs benefit millions of people who rarely, if ever, visit a National Park or designated historic site. These values include the sequestration of carbon that mitigates climate change, educational materials developed by NPS that bring National Parks and historic sites into classrooms throughout the USA, and even the use of National Parks as scenery used in movies and TV shows.

The book defines these many values from an economic perspective and for the first time provides methods to value them in monetary terms. It is these methods and approaches that will be of interest to professionals in state parks and county parks in the USA and park managers around the world. The methods proposed and illustrated with case studies in the book can be best viewed as a starting point for future research to refine these methods.

Despite the collective authors' estimates of nearly $100 billion in various benefits of National Parks and NPS programs, the book also identifies the several other values of National Parks and NPS programs that need to be studied in the future. These 'missing values' help set a research agenda not only for the NPS but also provide research topics for graduate students and professors the world over.

The research and ideas presented in this volume provide a critical step to understanding and quantifying the complete set of economic values associated with National Parks and programs. In turn, the work provides important input into the design of effective policy needed to fund and manage these areas. The chapters provide clear evidence that a multitude of benefits of National Parks are received by those that do not visit parks, suggesting that reliance solely on increasing visitor entrance fees may not be equitable. Finally, the book provides a useful array of innovative funding options for U.S. National Parks.

Linda J. Bilmes and John B. Loomis along with their coauthors have fundamentally advanced the state of our understanding of the value of the National Parks and the entire NPS to those who visit these jewels, are touched by NPS programs, or simply value the preservation of these natural lands. The book deserves a place on the shelf of all professionals who study and love the National Parks.

Catherine Kling
Tisch University Professor of Environmental,
Energy and Resource Economics,
Cornell University, Ithaca,
New York, USA.

Biographies

Editor biographies

Linda J. Bilmes, the Daniel Patrick Moynihan Senior Lecturer in Public Policy at the Harvard Kennedy School, is a leading expert on budgeting and public finance. She is a full-time faculty member, teaching budgeting, public finance, urban field labs, and teaching workshops in Harvard's training program for newly elected U.S. members of Congress and mayors. Bilmes was twice confirmed by the U.S. Senate, serving as Assistant Secretary and Chief Financial Officer of the U.S. Department of Commerce under President Bill Clinton. She was a member of the National Parks Conservation Association 'Second Century Commission' and served on the U.S. Department of Interior National Park Service Advisory Board from 2011 until 2017. She serves on the Board of Directors of the Institute for Veterans and Military Families at Syracuse University. She is Vice-chair of Economists for Peace and Security, and is the U.S. member of the United Nations Committee of Experts on Public Administration (CEPA), appointed by the Secretary-General. She serves on the Board of Directors of the Belfer Center for Science and International Affairs.

Professor Bilmes has authored or co-authored dozens of books, book chapters, papers, and articles on the costs of war, the value of public lands, conservation, and finance. She has testified to Congress on numerous occasions. Her books include the *New York Times* bestseller *The Three Trillion Dollar War: The True Cost of the Iraq Conflict* (with Joseph E. Stiglitz) and *The People Factor: Strengthening America by Investing in Public Service* (with W. Scott Gould). She has published widely in *The New York Times*, *The Boston Globe*, *Financial Times*, *Los Angeles Times*, *Harvard Business Review*, *Foreign Policy*, and *The Atlantic*. She is the recipient of the 2008 'Speaking Truth to Power' Award by the American Friends Service Committee. Bilmes was featured in the Academy Award–nominated documentary *No End in Sight*. She is a member of the Council on Foreign Relations and the United States member of the Committee of Experts on Public Administration of the United Nations and a Fellow of the National Academy of Public Administration.

Professor John B. Loomis is in the Department of Agricultural and Resource Economics, Colorado State University since 1993. Previously he was Associate Professor at the University of California-Davis. At the beginning of his career, he worked as an economist for two federal agencies in the U.S. Department of Interior. His primary research interests are in non-market valuation of natural resources such as recreation, instream flow, endangered species, and public lands. He is an expert in continent valuation method surveys. He has served as a Science Advisor to the Grand Canyon Monitoring and Research Center.

Professor Loomis has published more than 200 scientific articles in such journals as *Journal of Environmental Economics and Management*, *Journal of Forestry*, *Journal of Environmental Management*, *Ecological Economics*, and *Contemporary Economic Policy*. His books include *Integrated Public Lands Management*, *Determining the Economic Value of Water* (with R. Young, 2nd ed.), and *Environmental Policy Analysis for Decision Making* (with G. Helfand).

Professor Loomis' co-authored publications have received several awards including the 'Publication of Enduring Quality' from the Agricultural and Applied Economics Association. He is a Fellow of Association of Environmental and Resource Economists, as well as a Fellow in the Agricultural and Applied Economics Association. He is a Distinguished Scholar of the Western Agricultural Economics Association.

Contributors

Adam Banasiak, Master of Public Policy, Harvard Kennedy School, Harvard University, USA.

Linda J. Bilmes, Professor, Daniel Patrick Moynihan Senior Lecturer in Public Policy, Harvard Kennedy School, Harvard University, USA.

Michelle Haefele, Research Economist, Department of Agricultural and Resource Economics, Colorado State University, USA.

Jonathan Jarvis, Executive Director, Institute for Parks, People, and Biodiversity, University of California, Berkeley, USA and Former Director of National Park Service.

Lynne Koontz, Economist, Social Sciences Program, National Park Service.

Thomas J. Liu, former Research Associate, Harvard Kennedy School, Harvard University, USA.

John B. Loomis, Professor, Department of Agricultural and Resource Economics, Colorado State University, USA.

Timothy Marlowe, Research Director, National Opinion Research Center, University of Chicago, USA.

Catherine Cullinane Thomas, Economist, Social and Economic Analysis Branch, U.S. Geological Survey.

Stephen R. Thompson, Master of Public Policy, Harvard Kennedy School, Harvard University, USA.

1 Introducing the multiple values of National Parks, programs, and protected areas

John B. Loomis and Linda J. Bilmes

Introduction

The first National Park was established in 1872 when Congress designated Yellowstone as a National Park. This began a movement that has since spread worldwide, with more than 1,000 National Parks or preserves (https://www.nps.gov/aboutus/history.htm) created in over 100 countries. By itself, designating areas as National Parks is insufficient to protect the resources within the park unless there are personnel with authority to protect the resources and the budget to pay them. With Congress establishing more than a dozen new National Parks, it became apparent in 1916 that an agency was needed to carry out the purpose of Congressional designations. So in 1916 the US National Park Service (NPS) itself was established under the Department of the Interior. Its core mission is 'To conserve the scenery and natural and historic objects and wildlife therein and to provide for the enjoyment of the same in such a manner and by such means as will leave them unimpaired for the enjoyment of future generations'. This dual mandate (to conserve resources unimpaired *and* to provide for the enjoyment of the same) requires the NPS to manage a complex set of activities involving both conservation and visitors.

Today, the NPS oversees the system of National Park units covering more than 95 million acres as well as numerous programs within the parks. There are 418 NPS units in total, including 129 historical parks or sites, 88 national monuments, 60 National Parks, 25 battlefields or military parks, 19 preserves, 18 recreation areas, 14 seashores and lakeshores, and several other designations (collectively referred to hereafter as 'NPS units'). The agency employs 22,000 workers and engages 339,000 volunteers in the direct management of these places. Its annual budget in the fiscal year 2018 was $3.2 billion.

The NPS also promotes stewardship of natural, historic, cultural and recreational resources outside of NPS units. It does this by working with other federal jurisdictions, local and state governments, non-governmental organizations (NGOs), private landowners, and other stakeholders. Through its expertise in land management, historical preservation, and cultural steward-ship, the NPS helps to administer the National Register of Historic Places, National Heritage Areas, National Historic Landmarks, National Wild and Scenic Rivers, and multi-state regional trails (e.g., the Appalachian Trail in the eastern USA). In this way, the NPS plays a role in many aspects of national life and contributes in many ways to 'telling the American story'.

As one of the world's first government agencies dedicated to the preserva-tion of natural and cultural resources, the NPS has often served as a model for protected area management that many countries have adapted to their own histories and cultures. In the same way, the methods used to value NPS units and NPS programs can provide a useful guide for state agencies and for other countries around the world who want to estimate the economic value of their National Park and protected areas.

Valuing parks, wilderness, and other protected areas

This book develops a comprehensive framework to calculate the eco-nomic value of protected areas, with specific application to the US NPS. Our framework covers many different types of benefits arising from NPS units, including on-site visitation and other 'uses' of NPS units in education, movies/TV, and carbon sequestration. Our framework is unique in that it accounts for the benefits of NPS's cooperative interactions with stakehold-ers, which usually occur outside the boundaries of the NPS units themselves. The framework includes a graphical representation of the valuation model and a description of different types of value.

While we have applied this framework and accompanying methodologies to the US NPS, the approach taken in this book is equally applicable to pro-tected lands managed by other US agencies, such as the National Wildlife Refuges managed by the US Fish and Wildlife Service. Our valuation of the 95 million acres of NPS units implicitly includes 44 million acres that are Congressionally designated Wilderness within NPS units, i.e., roadless areas with no developments. Thus our valuation framework and methods apply equally well to designated Wilderness areas managed by the US Forest Service and the Bureau of Land Management as well as other similar road-less areas, e.g., Wilderness Study Areas and Primitive Areas. The valuation framework and methods are also appropriate for State Parks and the many US regional parks such as the Adirondack Regional Park in New York, as well as to counties with extensive parks/open space systems.

In addition, our valuation framework and methodologies can also be used to value protected areas outside the USA, either specific sites such as United Nations World Heritage sites on land or in the sea, e.g., Great Barrier Reef in Australia or entire national or regional park systems and marine preserves. Our methodologies could help agencies demonstrate that the protected areas they manage are of significant value not only to visitors but also to millions of people who may never visit the protected areas at all.

Classifying benefits of the National Parks and protected areas

There are several ways to categorize the economic benefits provided by the National Parks and protected areas. The first way is to identify those who benefit from them.

The most obvious beneficiaries of NPS units are those who visit NPS units. These visitors derive direct on-site 'recreation use benefits'. These types of benefits have been studied for decades in the USA and many countries around the globe. In the USA, direct recreation use benefits have been quantified at scales ranging from individual NPS units (e.g., Brookshire et al., 1976; Parson et al., 2009) to the entire NPS system (Nehr et al., 2013).

However, economists have demonstrated that part of the benefit of protected areas accrues to individuals who do not currently visit. Such people may benefit in three ways: (a) having the option to visit NPS units in the future; (b) satisfaction from knowing that NPS units continue to exist 'unimpaired', and (c) satisfaction from knowing that protection of NPS units today preserves these areas for the 'enjoyment of future generations'. The common terms for (a), (b), and (c) are option, existence, and bequest values, respectively. The sum of the direct on-site recreation visitor use benefits and the option value, existence value, and bequest value are referred to as total economic value (TEV). The off-site benefits (a), (b), and (c) are sometimes referred to as non-use or passive use values (Freeman, 2003).

Our analysis of TEV for US NPS units and programs provides a conservative estimate of $92 billion. Details of TEV study and the methods for estimating this value are explained in Chapter 2. This valuation represents a remarkable leveraging of the NPS's federal budget of approximately $3.2 billion, which has remained flat or declining for the past two decades (see Chapter 8).

The range of values discussed in this book is represented graphically in Figure 1.1. This chart, adapted from Francis Choi and Tim Marlowe (2012), provides an overview of the main functions of the NPS and the range of benefits it provides. This book focuses primarily on the types of value identified in the chart, using a variety of techniques to analyze and estimate values.

Operation and management of park units

This book addresses both the direct and passive use values of NPS units (the upper branch of Figure 1.1) created through two major categories: (1) production of goods and (2) production of services. Production of goods includes (a) resource extraction and intellectual property. Production of services includes (a) ecosystem services, (b) recreation visitation, and (c) human capital development.

Production of goods

Extraction: While NPS units produce goods, such as resource extraction and intellectual property, resource extraction is not a primary activity in

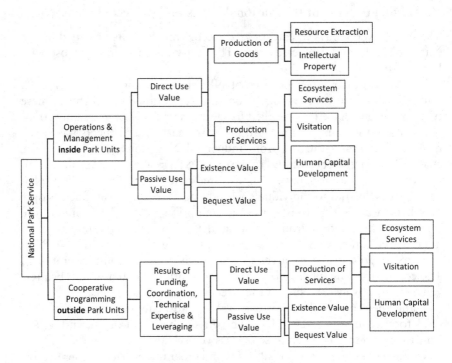

Figure 1.1 NPS total economic value framework

NPS units. Specifically, most NPS units prohibit extraction of resources such as logging and mining. However, some units provide for a modest amount of resource extraction through recreational fishing, limited hunting (e.g., Grand Teton NP), and in Alaska, limited subsistence uses. Alaska also contains several National Preserves that allow for sport hunting and commercial trapping (often regulated on these lands by the State of Alaska).

Intellectual property: On the other hand, NPS units support the creation of intellectual property in several ways. In general, NPS units provide an environment for scientific and historical research, and for creative media and the arts. In particular, NPS units provide natural laboratories or 'reference sites' that can also serve as 'control sites' in field experiments. For example, measurements of water quality taken in NPS units can be compared with water quality on sites that have mining, logging, or livestock grazing in order to determine the impacts of these activities on water quality. Further, protected areas also provide scientists with the opportunity to understand how natural processes operate when largely unimpeded by human disturbance. Scientists are now using at least 300 NPS units in a variety of research projects that will create intellectual property in one form or another.

Since 2000, there have been more than 28,000 scientific discoveries in NPS units, in fields ranging from biodiversity to bird migration to climate change (Robbins, 2016). Yellowstone National Park alone contains two-thirds of the world's geothermal features. Some of these discoveries have the potential to translate into important economic value. For example, a bacterium found in Mammoth Cave NP in Kentucky in 2002 has been used to develop new anti-cancer medicines based on angiogenesis[1]. There are numerous instances of such discoveries[2]. We were unable to estimate an economic value of scientific discoveries in this book. This is in part due to the well-known difficulty in valuing the benefits of basic scientific research such as the time lag between research and its commercial application (see Salter and Martin, 2001). However, scientific discoveries are undoubtedly of significant value and are an important area for future research.

The category of intellectual property also includes NPS units as an input to producing artwork, photographs, books, calendars, music, films, documentaries, commercials, and even music videos. Many of these have been created within or using the backdrop of National Parks[3]. This value is examined in Chapter 6 using the example of movies and television shows that were filmed partly in NPS units.

Production of services

Ecosystem services: There are numerous classifications of ecosystem services (see the Millennium Ecosystem Assessment, 2005, and Brown et al., 2007, for details). But a general one for evaluating the benefits of protected areas such as parks and protected areas (Dudley, Stolton, and Kettunen, 2013) uses three broad categories:

- Provisioning services: renewable resources such as fish, plants, soil, trees, water, and wildlife.
- Regulating services: includes purification of air/water, nutrient cycling, dispersal of seeds, erosion control, pest control, stabilization of climate (e.g., carbon sequestration), shoreline protection from storm surge, and reduction of the effects of floods.
- Cultural services: includes aesthetics, ecotourism, education, recreation, and spiritual values.

Of course, no single volume could accurately quantify the values for all these ecosystem services in the 418 NPS units. Therefore, the focus of this book is on a subset of all of these ecosystem services: (a) the value of ecotourism is discussed in Chapter 3. In Chapter 4 we calculate the value of carbon sequestration from NPS units in the continental USA. In Chapter 5, we provide estimates of the value of educational resources and programming provided by the NPS and its partners[4].

Recreation visitation: NPS units receive upwards of 300 million recreational visits each year. In recent years, visitation has exceeded 330 million. The benefit to those actually visiting NPS units have been well studied (see

Nehr et al., 2013, for a review and estimates for each major NPS unit) and is the focus of the NPS's own efforts to estimate some of the economic benefits of recreation.

Human capital development: Economists use the term 'human capital' to describe a wide range of educational investments that society makes in people. Such investments include formal schooling (preschool to postgraduate) as well as informal and life-long learning. As described in detail in Chapter 6, NPS provides numerous educational opportunities both directly (e.g., more than 660,000 children participated in 'Junior Ranger' programs in 2018) and indirectly through its work to create informational websites, teaching training materials, and its many partnerships and cooperative programs. Education is a merit good. Many people are willing to pay to provide not just for their own children but for others as well (Chapter 2 provides empirical evidence of this).

Passive use value

The lower branch of Operation and management of park units in Figure 1.1 is passive use value and its two elements, existence and bequest values. In Chapter 2, we derive the passive use value from the results of our TEV survey and previously published estimates of direct recreation use value of NPS units. This is the first systematic study of the passive use value of the entire set of 418 NPS units.

Cooperative programming

The lower branch of Figure 1.1 represents the second main vehicle through which NPS creates value. This vehicle is called 'cooperative programming'. This term refers to the NPS's role in integrating, assisting, and leveraging the efforts of numerous other stakeholders, many of whom exist outside of National Park units. These include thousands of public-private partnerships as well as state and local governments, educational institutions, concessioners, businesses, and friends groups. The NPS manages numerous programs that provide funding, technical assistance, and intellectual support to these stakeholders through formal and informal arrangements.

In Figure 1.1, we have identified four general categories of cooperative programming: funding, coordination and management, technical expertise, and organizational leveraging (Choi Marlowe, 2012).

Funding

The NPS administers a number of funding vehicles, such as the Land and Water Conservation Fund (LWCF) and the Historic Preservation Tax Incentives Program. LWCF programs provide matching grants to State and local entities for acquisition and development of public outdoor recreation areas and facilities as well as American Battlefield Protection. The Historic Preservation Tax Incentives Program works with the Internal Revenue Service and State Historic Preservation Offices (SHPOs) to promote the use of tax credits as a means of encouraging private property owners to rehabilitate historic buildings.

Coordination and management

The NPS acts as a kind of organizational 'glue' that helps to hold together numerous places which are patched together from a variety of (mostly contiguous) but multifold jurisdictions. For example, the Santa Monica Mountains National Recreation Area in Los Angeles is composed of 20 different landowner types, including federal, state, city, and county lands and private landowners, and more than 70 stakeholder groups. The NPS manages this complex arrangement, which contains a varied landscape that includes recreational hiking trails, archaeological sites, film studios, and coastline.

Some smaller NPS units require that the NPS coordinate among a number of jurisdictions. In most of these cases the NPS is not the primary landowner, but it still plays a significant role in managing and coordination. Examples of this include the Chesapeake Bay in Eastern Maryland and the Harbor Islands in Boston, Massachusetts. A more programmatic example of the coordination function of the NPS is the Hydropower Recreation Assistance Program. In this nationwide program, the NPS works with the Federal Energy Regulatory Commission to ensure that public interests in recreation and conservation are addressed during relicensing of private hydropower facilities.

Technical expertise

The NPS provides technical expertise in the management of botanical and wildlife species, land conservation, and historical research and preservation. For example, the NPS manages the National Center for Preservation Technology and Training, which assists many groups, including communities, museums, universities, and state, local, and international park agencies, with the technical challenges of preserving historic properties.

Organizational leveraging

The NPS also provides programmatic services in support of conservation by local communities, private landowners, and other stakeholders and partners. One example is the National Natural Landmarks Program, which recognizes sites that contain outstanding biological and geological resources. The sites are designated by the Secretary of Interior based on condition, illustrative character, rarity, diversity, historical use, and value to science and education.

Each one of these areas is studied in detail in Chapter 7. As illustrated in Figure 1.1, these four types of cooperative programs generate: (a) direct use values, e.g., visiting local historic sites and local natural areas that are outside of NPS units; and (b) passive use values, just knowing historic sites of local importance residing outside NPS units are protected for future generations.

A valuation continuum

Another perspective on economic values provided by NPS units is using a valuation continuum shown in Figure 1.2. Economists often use the terms 'values' and 'benefits' interchangeably. Economic values or benefits, whether market or non-market, are typically defined by economists as the maximum amount that an individual would pay rather than do without an increase in a particular good or service (Freeman, 2003). This definition is referred to as 'willingness to pay' (WTP) or consumer surplus. The WTP for the last unit of a market good consumed is equal to the price of that good. WTP is the federally approved measure of value used in cost-benefit analyses by a wide range of federal agencies. These agencies include the and US Bureau of Reclamation (US Water Resources Council, 1983), US Office of Management and Budget (1992), National Oceanic and Atmospheric Administration (Arrow et al., 1993), and the US Environmental Protection Agency (2010).

As shown in Figure 1.2, some benefits of NPS units are more readily quantifiable market-related values, such as the economic impact of ecotourism in the form of jobs, wages, and proprietor income (the subject of Chapter 3).

At the other end of the spectrum are cultural ecosystem services such as spiritual values, and values to ancestral native people who had been living on the land for centuries prior to designation as an NPS unit. Generally, these values are beyond monetary economic valuation. NPS units also provide non-human based intrinsic values to the plants and wildlife themselves that are also beyond economic valuation systems (see Gudmundsen and Loomis, 2005 and Rolston, 1988 for a review of intrinsic values of natural systems).

In between these two extremes are non-market economic values. The most obvious, and well studied, are the use benefits to visitors going to NPS units. Far less well studied are the benefits of knowing that NPS units exist in a protected state today (existence value) and for future generations (bequest value). The sum of the direct use values, option value, existence, and bequest values is the TEV, which is the focus of Chapter 2. A unique

Market Effects	Non-Market Economic Values		Non-economic Values
Prices, Ecotourism Jobs, profits	Benefits to the visitor themselves	Existence/Bequest values	Spiritual Benefits

<--->

Figure 1.2 Degree to which benefits of NPS units can be monetized

contribution of Chapter 2 is an estimation of TEV for NPS cooperative programs that provide protection of local historic sites and natural areas *outside* of NPS units.

Overview of chapters

This book is organized into nine chapters, each of which examines an approach to valuation of the different benefits provided by NPS units and programs.

Chapter 2: Measuring total economic value of NPS units and programs

In Chapter 2 we present the methodology and results of our new study on the TEV of NPS units and programs. We derive values for three different categories of NPS units and four groupings of NPS programs based on a peer-reviewed public valuation survey using WTP. This survey finds the American public has a TEV of $92 billion for NPS units and programs. Of this, approximately $62 billion is related to preservation of the NPS units themselves, and $30 billion to NPS cooperative programs. Of the $62 billion, based on other literature we infer that $33 billion of the $62 billion is related to passive use values such as existence and bequest values.

This valuation is conservative for several reasons. First, we chose WTP as the metric for this study as the best and most feasible method. When valuing improvements in the quantity or quality goods, the theoretically correct measure to use is the maximum WTP. However, if the valuation context is a degradation or removal of protection from existing NPS units or a reduction in existing NPS programs, then a more appropriate valuation context is the minimum amount an individual would accept, referred to as 'willingness to accept' or WTA (Freeman, 2003). Unfortunately, in practice it is very challenging to calculate a credible empirical measure of WTA based on surveys. As discussed more in detail in Chapter 2, there are several reasons for this. The primary reason is that a WTA question is very unfamiliar question in a survey. It is far more common for households to be asked in surveys and on ballots whether they would pay for a new or expanded public program, rather than what amount of money they would accept to give up that program.

Thus, WTP is often used as a lower bound proxy for WTA, with the caveat that several empirical studies (summarized by Horowitz and McConnell, 2002) and theoretical work (Hanemann, 1991) show that WTA for a loss can exceed WTP to avoid that loss by a substantial margin. This means that our valuation based on WTP likely understates the actual value that Americans place on the NPS.

WTP is also the appropriate measure of economic benefits to compare to the monetary cost of acquiring park lands/waters, the opportunity costs of foregone market development values arising from preservation of NPS units, or the budgetary costs of operating the park units. However, information on WTP is not always directly translatable into a financial measure of entrance/user fees[5].

Chapter 3: Economic contributions of visitor spending

The 330 million visitors to NPS units spend a total of $18.2 billion inside and within 60 miles of NPS units. This spending becomes revenues to organizations and businesses that support on-site recreation visitation to NPS units, i.e., hotels, restaurants, souvenir shops, guide services, etc. This spending ripples through the economy, generating positive economic contributions and regional economic impacts in the form of income, employment, and profits. While economists categorize these effects as regional economic contributions or impacts rather than economic benefits, i.e., WTP, these economic contributions matter greatly to the communities that receive them. As a result, the NPS devotes considerable effort to tracking the number of jobs that are related to its on-site recreation. The agency estimates that visitor spending inside and within 60 miles of NPS units supported more than 306,000 local jobs and contributed $35.6 billion to the US economy in 2018. The details of calculating these regional economic impacts in terms of jobs supported, wages, and taxes paid by businesses, as well as the limitations of this approach, are presented in this chapter.

Chapter 4: Carbon sequestration in the parks

In this chapter we illustrate the role of NPS units in providing ecosystem services, using the example of carbon sequestration, i.e., the process of removing carbon dioxide from the atmosphere and storing it in long-term mineral, organic, and oceanic reservoirs. Using five years of observed data, NPS boundary data, and land cover types, our study calculates the current tonnage and economic value of vegetative carbon sequestration services on all NPS units located in the continental USA. Our data indicates that NPS units are highly vegetated (85% of NPS lands). Using conservative assumptions, we find that at present average annual carbon sequestration on NPS lands amounts to 17.5 million metric tons of CO_2. Valuing this sequestered carbon using the 2013 federal interagency working group social cost of carbon damage price of $43/metric ton (updated to 2018 dollars) yields $752.5 million in benefits from NPS units. We also estimate the range of amounts of carbon that will be sequestered through 2050, based on examining land management practices and expected temperature change.

Chapter 5: Education and human capital

This chapter presents methods for valuing the comprehensive spectrum of educational benefits that the NPS provides, from preschool to life-long adult learning programs. At the national level, the NPS plays a role in education by developing curricula materials on important historical sites, e.g., Gettysburg, Ellis Island, as well as on the natural environment, e.g., information on wolves, bison, bird migration patterns, climate change, and natural landmarks. The NPS also runs programs such as 'Every Kid in a Park', which provides free entrance to NPS units, and programs for fourth graders by working with schools and families.

Additionally, many of the individual NPS units are engaged in educational programming, typically through cooperative efforts with a number of local partners. We illustrate these methods with an in-depth analysis of Golden Gate National Recreation Area in the San Francisco Bay Area and its partners. The results of this case study are generalized to arrive at an order of magnitude estimate of nationwide educational benefits provided by the NPS. Chapter 5 also presents methods that can be used to calculate the value of specific education programs.

Chapter 6: Intellectual property

One of the ways that the NPS creates value is by providing the raw material for the creation of intellectual property, such as scientific discovery and creative output. This chapter focuses on one example in the arts, the use of NPS units in films and TV shows. Many iconic films, and high-revenue earning 'blockbuster' movies, e.g., *Star Wars, Thelma and Louise, Forrest Gump,* and *E.T.,* and TV programs, e.g., *M.A.S.H.* and *Dr. Quinn Medicine Woman,* have included scenes filmed in NPS units. NPS units are an attractive location for several reasons, including their isolation and pristine condition as well as location and recognition value (e.g., the Statue of Liberty in the *Planet of the Apes*). In this way, NPS units make a direct contribution to the film and TV industries, which are among the most successful US exports worldwide.

However, location is only one input to the production of this intellectual property. In this chapter, we present several approaches to understanding the incremental value created by filming in the NPS units. Drawing on a sample of important movies and television shows filmed in NPS units, we use this chapter to illustrate the different ways that these locations may contribute to the value created by the filmmaker. We present a range of valuation models and apply the simple model to a case study of the value that Devils Tower National Monument contributed to the movie *Close Encounters of the Third Kind.*

Chapter 7: Valuing cooperative programming

Cooperative programming extends the reach of the NPS far beyond the borders of the NPS units. Several types of cooperative programming focus on historic site preservation and related training for non-NPS employees in historic preservation. Other types of cooperative programming focus on recreation, often related to local rivers and trails. Human capital development in the form of education for children and adults regarding the natural, historic, and cultural values embodied in NPS units is another type of cooperative programming that extends the NPS's reach into schools throughout the country. Some of this is delivered directly by NPS employees, but a great deal of it is provided by teachers using NPS-developed materials.

Cooperative programming is by far the smallest part of the NPS's budget at 1.7%. However, cooperative programming funding leverages millions of dollars in state and local government funding as well as non-profit stakeholder funding to accomplish far more than the NPS budget allocation implies. In Chapter 2 we provide results of a public survey-based estimate of the TEC of four broad categories of NPS programs ($30 billion). In Chapter 7, we look at a deeper qualitative and contextual analysis of cooperative programs. We provide a site-specific method to estimate the economic value of the NPS cooperative programming's contribution to multi-stakeholder projects. This chapter also illustrates how the NPS's cooperative programming has worked with multiple local and state governments as well as a variety of stakeholders on the large-scale Chesapeake Bay restoration on the east coast of the USA.

Chapter 8: Funding the next century of the NPS

The NPS is funded through a complex formula involving federal appropriations to each park unit, park entrance fees and concessions, and private funding raised by individual park donors. Unfortunately, the federal funding level of roughly $2.5 billion has been flat in real terms for the past two decades, despite the growing number of park units and visitors. Consequently, the NPS is fighting an uphill battle in its operational budget to keep the sites pristine and unspoiled. The agency has a mounting maintenance backlog that now stands at $12 billion. This chapter presents a number of proposals for reforming the NPS funding structure, including changes to how Congress funds the NPS, as well as in the administration of the NPS's own-source revenues such as concessions and fees, and private donations. We outline a series of reforms to improve the NPS's ability to finance infrastructure projects (which form the bulk of the maintenance backlog), including giving the NPS the ability to issue bonds.

Limitations of the research

This book presents a number of approaches to valuing NPS units and NPS cooperative programming. However, there are additional values of NPS units and NPS cooperative programming beyond those covered in this book that can be studied using different methods. For example, there is a growing body of literature showing the health benefits of outdoor recreation, including both physical and mental health benefits. In some areas, medical doctors prescribe outdoor exercise as the best and most cost-effective way to produce health value. Other types of value created by the NPS include a wider range of ecosystem services than are studied in this book. These ecosystem services include helping to safeguard endangered species, preventing soil erosion, and protecting watersheds (see Dudley, Stolton, and Kettunen, 2013 for a discussion of these ecosystem services and others in relation to protected areas in general). Rasker et al. (2013) have studied how the presence of protected areas such as National Parks contributes to the prosperity of local economies surrounding these protected areas. Many of these values are significant and deserve to be studied. We hope this book will encourage others to do so in the future.

Double counting

There are several other challenges in measuring the benefits of NPS units and NPS cooperative programming. The first is to provide as comprehensive a measure as possible without double counting some of the same categories of benefits multiple times. Chapter 2 provides a single valuation effort at the national level that conservatively estimates $92 billion for the set of seven benefits—three for different types of NPS units and four distinct values for NPS cooperative programs. In Chapters 3, 4, 5, and 6 we provide detailed case studies of a subset of benefits such as ecotourism (Chapter 3), carbon sequestration (Chapter 4), education (5), and intellectual property (Chapter 6). The purpose of these case studies is to illustrate topic-specific methods and provide more in-depth estimates of specific benefits of the NPS. The reader is cautioned against adding the benefit estimates from the case studies to the comprehensive benefit measure provided in Chapter 2 as there is a potential for double counting.

Notes

1 See 102nd General Meeting of the American Society for Microbiology, May 19–23, 2002, in Salt Lake City, Utah. https://www.eurekalert.org/pub_releases/2002-05/asfm-bdi051402.php
2 For example, Yellowstone NP hot springs contain a novel positive-strand RNA virus that provide scientific understanding of the relationships between RNA viruses from the three domains of cellular life (Bolduc et al., 2012). It is unknown how long such an important finding manifests itself in medical treatments.
3 See for example, *Painters of Grand Tetons National Park* (Poulton and Poulton, 2015) a collection of 400 paintings and photographs that feature the Grand Tetons/Jackson Hole landscape.
4 For an overview of methods and some examples of regulating ecosystem services in protected areas see Badura and Kettunen (2013). For details of measuring the economic values of water related ecosystem services see Young and Loomis (2014).

5 For example, if the average visitor's maximum WTP is $102 per visit to a typical National Park unit (Neher et al., 2013), this does not mean the NPS can charge each visitor $102. First, because WTP is an average number, by definition half the visitors would pay $102 or more per visit, but half would pay less. Hence charging $102 per visit might result in half as much visitation, depending on the shape of the demand curve for a specific NPS unit. Second, while visitors might pay $102 for the first visit, if individuals make multiple trips to the same National Park, they are less likely to pay $102 for the last visit. Rather the WTP for the last unit consumed (e.g., a visit) is likely to be just slightly more than the visitor's travel costs.

References

Arrow, K., R. Solow, P. Portney, E. Leamer, R. Radner, and H. Schuman. 1993. Report of the NOAA Panel on Continent Valuation. http://www.economia.unimi b.it/DATA/moduli/7_6067/materiale/noaa%20report.pdf. (Also published in *Federal Register* January 15, 1993, 4601–4614.)

Badura, T. and M. Kettunen. 2013. Regulating services and related goods. In M. Kettunen and P. ten Brink, eds. *Social and Economic Benefits of Protected Areas: An Assessment Guide.* New York, NY: Routledge.

Brookshire, D., B. Ives, and W. Schulze. 1976. Valuation of aesthetic preferences. *Journal of Environmental Economics and Management* 3: 325–346.

Brown, T., J. Bergstrom, and J. Loomis. 2007. Defining, valuing, and providing ecosystem goods and services. *Natural Resources Journal* 47(2): 329–376.

Choi, F. and T. Marlow. 2012. *The Value of America's Greatest Idea: Framework for Total Economic Valuation of National Park Service Operations and Assets and Joshua Tree National Park Total Economic Value Case Study.* Cambridge, MA: Harvard Kennedy School of Government.

Dudley, N., S. Stolton, and M. Kettunen. 2013. Contextual guidance. In M. Kettunen and P. ten Brink, eds. *Social and Economic Benefits of Protected Areas: An Assessment Guide.* New York, NY: Routledge.

Freeman, A. M. 2003. *The Measurement of Environmental and Resource Values: Theory and Methods,* Second Edition. Washington, DC: Resources for the Future. 491 pp.

Gudmundsen, S. and J. Loomis. 2005. Tracking the intrinsic value of wilderness. In K. Cordell, J. Bergstrom, and J. Bowker, eds. *The Multiple Values of Wilderness.* State College, PA: Venture Publishing Inc.

Hanemann, M. 1991. Willingness to pay and willingness to accept: how much can they differ? *American Economic Review* 81(3): 635–647.

Horowitz, J. and K. McConnell. 2002. A review of WTA/WTP Studies. *Journal of Environmental Economics and Management* 44(3): 426–447.

Loomis, J. 2002. *Integrated Public Lands Management: Principles and Applications to National Forests, Parks and Wildlife Refuges, and BLM Lands.* New York, NY: Columbia University Press.

Millennium Ecosystem Assessment. 2005. *Ecosystems and Human Well-being: Synthesis.* Washington, DC: Island Press.

Neher, C., J. Duffield, and D. Patterson. 2013. Valuation of National Park System visitation: the efficient use of count data models, meta-analysis, and secondary visitor survey data. *Environmental Management* 52(3): 683–698.

Parsons, G., A. Kang, C. Leggett, and K. Boyle. 2009. Valuing beach closures on the Padre Island National Seashore. *Marine Resource Economics* 24(3): 213–235.

Poulton, D. and J. Poulton. 2015. *Painters of Grand Tetons National Park*. Layton, UT: Gibbs Smith Publishing.

Rasker, R., P. Gude, and M. Delorey 2013. The effect of protected federal lands on economic prosperity in the non-metropolitan west. *Journal of Regional Analysis and Policy* 43(2): 110–122.

Robbins, J. August 24, 2016. Science in the Wild: The Legacy of the US National Park System. *YaleEnvironment360*. Yale School of Forestry and Environmental Studies. https://e360.yale.edu/features/science_in_the_wild_legacy_of_the_us_na tional_park_system.

Rolston, H. 1988. *Environmental Ethics: Duties to and Values in the Natural World*. Philadelphia, PA: Temple University Press.

Salter, A. and B. Martin. 2001. The economic benefits of publicly funded basic research: a critical review. *Research Policy* 30(3): 509–532.

US Environmental Protection Agency. 2010. *Guidelines for Preparing Economic Analyses*. Washington, DC.

US Office of Management and Budget. 1992. Circular No. A-94 Revised. Memorandum for Heads of Executive Departments and Establishments, Guidelines and Discount Rates for Benefit-Cost Analysis of Federal Programs. https://www.whitehouse.gov/omb/circulars_a094/.

US Water Resources Council. 1983. *Economic and Environmental Principles and Guidelines for Water and Related Land Resources Implementation Studies*. Washington, DC.

Young, R. and J. Loomis. 2014. *Determining the Economic Value of Water: Concepts and Methods*, Second Edition. Washington, DC: Resources for the Future Press.

2 Total economic valuation of the National Park units and National Park Service cooperative programs

Results of a survey of the American public

Michelle Haefele, John B. Loomis, and Linda J. Bilmes

Introduction

This chapter describes the first-ever estimate of the total economic value (TEV) of the entire National Park Service (NPS) including the lands managed by the NPS and the programs the agency administers. The results of this study provide lower bound estimates that the American public values units of the National Park System at $62 billion, with $23.3 billion for nature-focused National Park Service units (NPS units), $18.3 billion for history-focused NPS units, and $20.4 billion for water-focused NPS units. Overall NPS programs were valued by the American public at $30 billion, with $6.6 billion for history programs, $2 billion for NPS-facilitated transfer of lands to communities for recreation, $7.2 billion for protection of natural landmarks of significance to local communities, and $14.2 billion for NPS programs aimed at schoolchildren. This chapter details the concepts and methods used to estimate these values.

Over the past 30 years, a number of studies have looked at the amount the public would pay for individual national park units or specific benefits of the NPS system. These studies utilize a range of attributes, values, and methodologies. For example, a previous analysis of NPS visitation data using a travel demand method found a median value of $108 per day (Neher et al., 2013) for recreation at units of the National Park system throughout the country. Duffield (2006) estimates both use and nonuse values for a National Park and National Recreation Area within the Colorado River watershed. Schulze et al. (1983, 1985) used contingent valuation to estimate the value of air quality (visibility) in the National Parks in the Southwest (Grand Canyon NP, Mesa Verde NP, and Zion NP). Other studies focus on the economic contribution and economic impact (jobs, income, tax revenue) of visitor spending at National Parks. Chapter 3 of this book presents the latest estimates of these studies for the NPS as a whole.

The study described in this chapter is the first to look at the NPS system as a whole. It addresses the broader question of the TEV to the American public, not only visitors, but also non-visiting households. Thus this TEV is composed of both on-site use value and off-site passive-use values such as existence and bequest values (Krutilla, 1967). Existence value is the utility or benefit that accrues to an individual from simply *knowing* that a resource (such as a National Park) exists, even if the individual never expects to visit or see or otherwise use the resource. Bequest value measures the benefit or utility an individual enjoys from knowing that a resource will be preserved for future generations.

Our TEV study may also serve as a template for managers of state parks, regional parks, and international protected areas worldwide who want to estimate the TEV of their entire network of state parks or a country's net-work of protected areas. The overall approach would be similar to what is presented in this chapter, although the details of the method would of course have to be tailored to the specific context of each state or country.

Our study began with the TEV framework by Choi and Marlowe (2012), which was described in Chapter 1. Their work outlined a comprehensive framework for valuing the NPS—including economic impacts, intangible benefits from cooperative programs, and non-market value. We believe the Choi and Marlowe framework could be adapted to state parks or a country's system of protected areas. Therefore, the Choi and Marlowe framework could serve as a useful starting point for TEV study of a state's or country's park system.

Economic valuation methodology

Empirical measures of TEV

Most of the economic value associated with the NPS is what economists call *non-market value*. There are no formal markets for such things as public lands recreation opportunities, clean air, and endangered species, so there are no market-clearing 'prices' for these goods as there are for market goods such as food or clothing.

However, the same economic principles used to value market goods can be applied to estimate the economic values (including direct-use and passive-use values) of non-market goods. For example, economists measure economic value as the maximum amount that an individual would pay rather than do without a particular good or service. This definition is referred to as 'willingness to pay' (WTP) and is the federally approved measure of value used in cost-benefit analyses by many federal agencies. These agencies include the U.S. Bureau of Reclamation (Welsh et al., 1997; U.S. Water Resources Council, 1983), U.S. Office of Management and Budget (1992), National Oceanic and Atmospheric Administration (Arrow et al., 1993), and U.S. Environmental Protection Agency (2010).

WTP is the most appropriate estimate of value to use for additions to the National Park System because the public does not yet have or 'own' these potential new additions. However, given the overall budget situation facing the USA, and NPS in particular, along with our own pre-testing of an early version of this survey, it was more believable that there would be *cuts* to NPS units and NPS programs. Therefore the survey was based on the idea of avoiding cuts to the acreage of NPS units and NPS programs.

When estimating the value associated with taking away a resource that the public already 'owns' or is entitled to, economists generally use the concept of minimum 'willingness to accept' (WTA) (Freeman, 2003). This is the minimum payment a person would accept in exchange for a decrease in a good or service. Given that the goal of this study was to estimate the TEV of all existing National Parks that the public already 'owns' and has a legal right to, WTA would be the theoretically correct approach to estimating TEV when a reduction is proposed, however, there are some barriers to using WTA.

Specifically, there are several drawbacks to asking WTA in a survey of the general public. First, economists have had limited success empirically estimating WTA in non-market valuation surveys. This may be due in part to the fact that it is rare for people to actually be asked if they are willing to give up an existing public resource in exchange for some amount of money (perhaps in the form of a tax refund). It is much more common, and therefore more familiar, for surveys to ask households if they would pay *additional* taxes of some form (sales, property, income) to provide *more* of a public good such as expanding schools, parks, open space, roadways, etc. In addition, a review of the literature on reported WTP and WTA, Horowitz and McConnell (2002) found that WTA was frequently twice as large as WTP for all types of goods, and as much as 10 times larger for non-market goods. Several explanations for this effect have been offered. These include the binding budget constraint that applies to WTP but not to WTA. As Freeman (2003: 87) summarizes: 'These differences (between WTP and WTA) can be explained by the absence of close substitutes in the case of unique and perhaps irreplaceable resources…'. Hanemann (1991) also showed that if a person does not think there are good substitutes for the natural resource that he or she could buy with the money provided as compensation, WTA could be larger than WTP by a sizeable amount. This very large disparity between WTP and WTA often cast doubts on the estimates of WTA as a believable estimate of value (Horowitz and McConnell, 2003: 544).

Thus, like most economists, we have used WTP to retain the current National Parks and NPS programs. This is the conservative approach, but one recommended by the Blue Ribbon Panel (Arrow et al., 1993) for performing studies such as ours. Therefore our final estimates almost certainly generate results that are an underestimate of the TEV of the entire the National Park System and NPS programs.

Empirical methods used for this study

As noted in the preceding, the majority of the economic value associated with National Parks and NPS programs is non-market value, which needs to be measured using techniques that do not rely on market prices. Measuring non-market values can be done either indirectly or directly. *Indirect* methods infer the value of the good in question by observing consumer behavior. These are called *revealed preference* methods because the value is revealed by the actual purchases the consumer makes, thereby indicating their preference for the good. For example, a common method to estimate recreation values uses the cost of a visit (transportation costs) as a price along with the number of trips taken to trace out a demand curve, from which the value of the recreation experience can be calculated (Champ et al., 2003). This technique is commonly known as the travel cost or travel demand method.

Direct methods to measure non-market values are referred to as *stated preference* methods because such techniques involve directly asking consumers to state what they would pay for a non-market good. Stated preference methods are the only methods that can estimate passive-use values (Freeman, 2003) because people who have passive-use values for a resource, such as existence and bequest values, rarely manifest these values in any traceable behavior.

The two main types of stated preference methods are contingent valuation (CVM) and choice experiments (CE). CE are sometimes referred to as contingent choice, conjoint method, or stated choice. In the CVM method survey respondents are asked to indicate their willingness to pay for a non-market good such as a recreation experience or passive-use values such as existence value, option value or bequest value (Mitchell and Carson 1989). In the CE method survey respondents are asked to choose from a set of alternative scenarios that vary in the level of several attributes, one of which is the price or cost (Louviere et al., 2000; Bennett and Blamey, 2001).

The CE method has two practical advantages over CVM in our particular study. First, the CE WTP question format is more akin to the consumers' choices in a market. Specifically, CE offers respondents more than one 'take it or leave it' bundle of attributes that is typical in many CVM studies. Instead, CE respondents are asked to choose their most preferred from a set of alternatives (Freeman 2003). This exercise most closely mimics the act of purchasing a market good, where consumers choose from among several alternative products, weighing the various product's attributes (one of which is the cost) to determine the most preferred (Louviere et al., 2000; Freeman, 2003; Hensher et al., 2005).

Second, CE is capable of gathering more information from survey respondents. When analyzing the results of choice experiments, researchers are able to estimate not only the total value, but also the incremental WTP for each of the non-monetary attributes of each alternative (Freeman, 2003). Knowing what the economic value of each attribute is for NPS programs and NPS units provides information as to what type of NPS programs or NPS units are most valuable to the public.

Boyle and Markowski (2003) and Turner (2012) both recommend using CE when estimating economic values for NPS resources. Both also describe a comprehensive framework for developing estimates of value for National

Park System resources and National Park programs. Based on the recommendations and on the advantages of the choice experiment format for valuing the many different dimensions of the National Park System, we selected the CE method to apply for our study.

Questionnaire design and survey implementation

Questionnaire development

Given the scale and complexity of the public good being valued, we believed it was essential to solicit input from potential respondents in order to ensure that our questionnaire design was clear and the questions phrased in clear, unambiguous language. The initial survey design was thus refined over several months with the aid of nine focus groups and six individual interviews conducted in Fort Collins and Denver, Colorado; Woburn, Massachusetts; and South San Francisco, California. The focus groups each included about a dozen people randomly selected as representative of the general population. We told the participants that the purpose of the focus group was to help design a survey. We handed out a page of the survey and asked participants to read it, mark up anything that was not clear, and answer the questions on the page. The moderator then went around the room and asked participants to explain their concerns with the text or the questions. This process was repeated for each page of the survey. The focus groups usually met for about two hours. We ran separate focus groups for the National Park units and for National Park programs so that adequate time was available to discuss each aspect of the survey in detail.

The input from these focus groups was extremely helpful in designing a survey that was comprehensible for most people and contained plausible valuation scenarios in light of the budget issues facing the NPS. Based on responses from the first few focus groups we changed from valuing an increase in park lands and expansion of NPS programs to valuing the prevention of cuts to programs and the sale of sites and lands. Cuts or transfer of federal lands such as National Parks has been proposed a few times by one or more outside groups (e.g., Sagebrush Rebellion) over the past three decades so it was deemed a plausible scenario.

We also decided to design a single 12-page survey that included both National Park units and NPS programs rather than split the sample and use separate survey versions for parks and programs. This also ensured that respondents were valuing cuts to National Park units and NPS programs as separate and distinct elements, and that they had to consider the cost of both scenarios relative to their household budget when answering the two WTP questions. (See https://heep.hks.harvard.edu/files/heep/files/dp71_haef ele-loomis-bilmes.pdf for a copy of the full questionnaire.)

The first section of the questionnaire contained a brief description of the NPS with examples of the various types of National Parks and NPS programs. We divided the National Parks into three broad categories: (1) National Parks that focus on the preservation of nature and nature-based recreation; (2) parks that focus on the preservation of American history and culture or the commemoration and remembrance of significant events and people; and (3) parks that focus on protecting shorelines and bodies of water. For nature-focused and water-focused parks we used acres as the unit of measure, but for the historic parks we used the number of sites. The reason for this is that the history-focused parks are often very small, representing less than 1% of the total NPS acreage, but account for 57% of total NPS units.

The NPS administers several dozen programs. For the purposes of this survey, we group all these programs into four major programmatic areas: conservation, education, historical preservation, and recreation. Specifically, our four main NPS program categorical areas are: (1) programs that focus on the preservation of local historic buildings and sites; (2) programs that create and improve recreation opportunities for communities; (3) programs that focus on the protection of natural environments; and features that are important to communities and (4) educational programs that help children and adults learn about historical, cultural, and environmental topics. Each of these is described in terms of annual outputs. Table 2.1 shows the park units and program attributes along with the specific metrics used for each (the full descriptions can be found in the example questionnaire located at https://heep.hks.harvard.edu/files/heep/files/dp71_haefele-loomis-bilmes.pdf). In the questionnaire, these divisions are denoted using icons and colors that are carried through the questionnaire.

The second section of the questionnaire consisted of 12 Likert-scale style questions designed to elicit respondents' general attitude toward the NPS, National Parks, and outcomes of the NPS programs. This was followed by a detailed description of the National Parks and NPS programs and the valuation questions. The scenario we presented to respondents was a proposal to sell some National Park lands and/or sites and cut some NPS programs as a response to large federal government budget deficits. This was credible to respondents and has some validity as there are occasional political proposals along these lines.

To minimize the potential for hypothetical bias by respondents unintended overstatement of their WTP, two steps were taken. First, the scenario description of cuts to park units or programs was followed by a 'budget reminder' that asked respondents to consider their household budget as well as the combined cost of both of their preferred alternative for NPS units and programs. The second was a reminder to think about the other goods they could buy with their money or government programs that they might prefer to spend the money on. These reminders are recommended by the Blue Ribbon Panel on CVM (Arrow et al., 1993) and have been shown to reduce hypothetical bias (Cummings and Taylor 1999, Carlsson et al. 2005, Silva et al. 2011).

Table 2.1 Attribute descriptions

Types of National Parks	Metric
National Park areas that focus on the preservation of nature and nature-based recreation (e.g., National Parks, some National Monuments, National Preserves, National Parkways, National Scenic Trails and some National Recreation Areas)	Acres: 79,096,632
National Park areas that focus on the preservation of American history and culture or the commemoration and remembrance of significant events and people (e.g., National Historic Sites, National Battlefields, National Memorials and some National Monuments)	Park units: 226
National Park areas that focus on protecting shorelines and bodies of water (e.g., National Lakeshores on the Great Lakes, National Seashores, National Rivers and some National Recreation Areas).	Acres: 4,818,275

Park acreage, number of sites and program outputs are all from various NPS publications or personal communication with NPS from 2012 to 2013.

Types of NPS programs outside of National Parks	Metric
Preservation of local historic buildings and sites that commemorate American history and culture or significant events and people	Annual number of historic sites protected: 2000
Creation and improvement of recreation opportunities for communities	Annual number of acres transferred: 2700
Protection of natural environments and features that are important to communities	Annual number of sites designated: 114
Educational programs that help children and adults learn about historical, cultural, and environmental topic	Children attending programs annually: 4,100,000

Acreage, number of sites, and program outputs were based on NPS publications and/ or personal communication with NPS personnel from 2012 to 2013. Children attending educational programs was calculated based on the 2012 NPS estimate and materials prepared by Dr. Milton Chen, Edutopia, February 2013.

We presented respondents with two choice questions—one on National Parks the other on NPS programs, each consisting of three options. The status-quo (or 'do nothing') option proposes the highest levels of cuts, with a tax cost of $0. The middle option proposes smaller cuts and some annual tax cost. The third option for each choice question preserves all current parks or programs with the highest annual cost to the household. Varying levels of cuts to the park and program categories described above were used as the non-price attributes (three for parks, four for programs). See Figure 2.1 for an example of one of the 16 versions of the National Parks Areas choice matrix and Figure 2.2 for the corresponding choice matrix for the National Park Programs in Communities (they are shown in black and white here, but were in color in the actual survey booklet).

OPTIONS FOR NATIONAL PARK AREAS

Options A and B are proposals to sell land in some or all of each type of National Park area.
Option C would retain all current National Park areas.
The option chosen by a majority of households will be carried out, and all households will pay the amount specified. There is no right or wrong answer, please choose the option that is best for you.
At the bottom of this table, please check the boxes to indicate your <u>most preferred</u> option and your <u>least preferred</u> option:

	Option A Sale of some land in all parks	Option B Smaller land sales in some or all parks	Option C No sale of park lands
National Park areas that focus on the preservation of nature and nature-based recreation.	Acres sold: 19,774,159 25% Acres kept: 59,322,474 75%	Acres sold: 7,909,663 10% Acres kept: 71,186,969 90%	No sale – keep all 79,096,632 acres
National Park areas that focus on the preservation of American history and culture.	Historic sites sold: 57 25% Historic sites kept: 170 75%	No sale – keep all 226 sites	No sale – keep all 226 sites
National Park areas that focus on protecting shorelines and bodies of water.	Acres sold: 1,927,310 40% Acres kept: 2,890,965 60%	Acres sold: 722,741 15% Acres kept: 4,095,534 85%	No sale – keep all 4,818,275 acres
Your household's annual tax cost for each of the next 10 years:	**for Option A:** $0	**for Option B:** $150	**for Option C:** $400
1. Select Your Single <u>Most</u> Preferred Option:	Option A ☐	Option B ☐	Option C ☐
2. Select Your Single <u>Least</u> Preferred Option:	Option A ☐	Option B ☐	Option C ☐

Figure 2.1 Example of the National Parks choice matrix

We chose an annual increase in federal income taxes as a realistic means of payment to prevent the sale of National Parks or to avoid cuts to NPS programs. Taxes sometimes cause survey respondents to react negatively and reject paying anything, not because they have a true zero value of the good, but because of attitudes toward the federal government in general or objections to paying by means of taxes for anything. This is called a *protest response*. While these can be problematic to deal with, taxes as a means of payment can also can ensure that non-protest responses are valid willingness to pay responses because respondents are likely to see their answers as consequential to the amount of taxes they would pay (Carson and Groves, 2007). We decided this beneficial property of consequentiality outweighed the potential for protest responses. Therefore we asked protest check questions to determine if the reason for a zero willingness to pay was valid (National Park areas are not worth that much to me or I cannot afford to pay) versus other reasons indicating an aversion to paying taxes.

The final overall survey design consisted of 16 versions of the questionnaire which varied the percentage of cuts to National Parks and NPS programs, and the cost of the options (amount of the associated increase in income taxes the respondent would be asked to pay). The options with the maximum sale of National Parks and maximum cuts to NPS programs (described in the survey as the status quo) vary only in the level of cuts—ranging from 20–40%—and the price is always zero. The option with no sale of National Parks and no cuts to NPS programs has the highest price and varies only in the household cost—ranging from $115 to $600 (the amount of land sold or cuts to programs is always zero). The middle option has smaller cuts to parks and programs (0–20%) and lower household costs ($15–$100). The combinations of attributes and cost levels (a more complex version of a main effects orthogonal design) was designed by Dr. Barbara Kanninen of BK Econometrics.

Each of the choice questions followed the same format, incorporating icons and color codes used in the description of National Parks and NPS program types, along with color-coded pie charts graphically illustrating the reductions (sale of National Parks or cuts to annual NPS program outputs). We asked respondents to indicate their *most preferred* option and their *least preferred* option. This format maximizes the amount of information we obtain from a given respondent. Figures 2.1 and 2.2 provide examples of one of the 16 park unit and NPS program valuation scenarios, respectively.

The valuation section concluded with three follow-up questions. The first question asked respondents how certain they were that their answers would be used to make policy decisions, the second asked how certain they were that they would actually have to pay the proposed tax. Answers to these two questions help us assess whether respondents' perceptions of the questionnaire were consequential to real-world decisions directly affecting them (Carson and Groves, 2007; Vossler and Evans, 2009). Responses to this first question in the focus groups indicated that some focus group participants

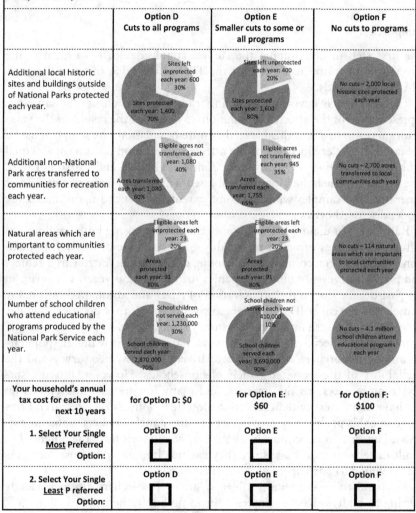

OPTIONS FOR PROGRAMS IN COMMUNITIES

Options D and E are proposals to make cuts or reductions to some or all types of programs in local communities.

Option F would keep all programs in local communities at their current levels.

The option chosen by a majority of households will be carried out, and all households will pay the amount specified. There is no right or wrong answer, please choose the option that is best for you.

At the bottom of this table, please check the boxes to indicate your most preferred option and your least preferred option:

	Option D Cuts to all programs	Option E Smaller cuts to some or all programs	Option F No cuts to programs
Additional local historic sites and buildings outside of National Parks protected each year.	Sites left unprotected each year: 600 — 30%; Sites protected each year: 1,400 — 70%	Sites left unprotected each year: 400 — 20%; Sites protected each year: 1,600 — 80%	No cuts – 2,000 local historic sites protected each year
Additional non-National Park acres transferred to communities for recreation each year.	Eligible acres not transferred each year: 1,080 — 40%; Acres transferred each year: 1,080 — 60%	Eligible acres not transferred each year: 945 — 35%; Acres transferred each year: 1,755 — 65%	No cuts – 2,700 acres transferred to local communities each year
Natural areas which are important to communities protected each year.	Eligible areas left unprotected each year: 23 — 20%; Areas protected each year: 91 — 80%	Eligible areas left unprotected each year: 23 — 20%; Areas protected each year: 91 — 80%	No cuts – 114 natural areas which are important to local communities protected each year
Number of school children who attend educational programs produced by the National Park Service each year.	School children not served each year: 1,230,000 — 30%; School children served each year: 2,870,000 — 70%	School children not served each year: 410,000 — 10%; School children served each year: 3,690,000 — 90%	No cuts – 4.1 million school children attend educational programs each year
Your household's annual tax cost for each of the next 10 years	for Option D: $0	for Option E: $60	for Option F: $100
1. Select Your Single Most Preferred Option:	Option D ☐	Option E ☐	Option F ☐
2. Select Your Single Least Preferred Option:	Option D ☐	Option E ☐	Option F ☐

Figure 2.2 Example of the NPS programs choice matrix

definitely felt their answers would affect policy, to the point of expressing they were worried that the government would use responses to their surveys to decide whether and how much to reduce National Parks. This suggested that they did find the questions consequential. The third question was designed to allow us to determine the whether the reason for a zero bid was a 'protest zero response' or a genuine reflection of a zero value for changes in the quantity of NPS units or inability to pay.

Sample design

The first step in determining the survey sample design is to identify the affected population. In the case of the TEV of the NPS, this population is all U.S. households.

The next step is devising a sampling frame that will ensure the sample is representative of the affected population. In order for the results of the valuation survey to be generalizable to the entire population, the sample must be unbiased, i.e., every member of the affected population must have an equal probability of being selected for the sample (Mitchell and Carson, 1989). The extent to which the sample is unbiased will depend upon the method of generating the sample (which to some extent will depend upon the survey mode, discussed below).

Random digit dialing (RDD) of phone area codes using both landline and cell phone prefixes provides reasonably good coverage of the U.S. population. RDD has been commonplace among university survey research centers and private survey sampling companies for the past 30 years. However, in the past decade due to the proliferation of RDD and automated calls many households use caller ID and do not answer numbers they do not recognize. As such the response rate of phone surveys can be low.

In the past decade, internet surveys have been growing in popularity among researchers due to their relatively low cost per survey and the availability of pre-recruited panels of households. However, internet surveys require access to the internet, and many low-income households do not have computers with access to the internet. Some survey research firms overcome this problem by providing potential panel members with computers and internet connections. Nonetheless, such panels have the potential to result in self-selection bias (since they exclude households whose members are unwilling to participate in internet surveys).

To avoid these sampling problems, survey researchers are increasingly turning to address-based samples. Our sampling frame consists of all U.S. households with valid addresses contained in the U.S. Postal Service Delivery Sequence file. According to the Wyoming Survey and Analysis Center, 'This is the sampling frame that is recognized to provide the best coverage of all households in a geographic area of interest at reasonable cost.' The Center calculated that random samples yielding 600 completed surveys '...will yield margins of error of about ±4 percentage points, with 95% confidence.' (Wyoming Survey and Analysis Center, 2013).

Survey mode

Survey mode refers to the means by which the survey questionnaire is delivered to potential respondents. Modes include in-person interviews, mailed questionnaires, phone surveys, and more recently online or some combination of modes. Some survey modes, such as in-person surveys, may produce inflated willingness to pay values due to respondents wishing to please the interviewer (Leggett et al. 2003). Other modes may result in unrepresentative samples (e.g., an online-only survey may underrepresent households without internet access). Thus, for our survey we used a mixed online and mail mode because a great deal of recent research (Grandjean et al., 2009; Taylor et al., 2009; Poole and Loomis, 2010; Kaplowitz et al., 2004; Evans and Mathur, 2005; Lindhjem and Navrud, 2011; Berrens et al., 2004) has indicated that a mixed-mode approach (combining online, mail, and/or phone) may increase response rates and the representativeness of the final sample.

Survey implementation and response rates

This chapter combines the results of two separate rounds of surveying done in 2013–2014 and 2015. The procedures followed for the two survey rounds were nearly identical. All members of the survey sample were initially invited to participate in the survey by means of a paper letter on letterhead with both Colorado State University and the University of Wyoming mailed to their home address. The letter provided a web link to the survey in the form of a unique URL. A few weeks later, non-respondents in both rounds were mailed a second paper letter, which repeated their survey web link, but also included the 12-page color paper questionnaire (with a postage paid return envelope) and a two-dollar bill as an incentive/reward.

In the first round (2013–2014), we contacted non-respondents for whom phone numbers were available by phone with a reminder message. A third reminder letter with a web link was sent a few days later. The final contact in the first round included a second paper questionnaire and web link mailed to non-respondents. In the second round (2015), we sent a reminder postcard to non-respondents about two weeks after the first paper questionnaire was mailed. Then two waves of phone calls were made—one immediately after the reminder postcard and the second after a second paper survey was mailed about a month later.

The 2013–2014 sample included 1,630 valid addresses with 317 questionnaires completed (for a 19% response rate). The 2015 sample included 2,246 valid addresses and 391 completed questionnaires (17% response rate). We pooled the data from the two survey rounds after determining that the samples were not statistically different from each other and the results reported in the remainder of this chapter reflect the pooled sample. The final sample of 708 observations is well over the minimum sample size of 500 that is recommended for conjoint/choice experiments (Orme, 2010).

The overall response rate of 18% is lower than ideal, but similar to other longer stated preference survey response rates (Stratus Consulting, 2015).

In addition, the National Research Council (NRC) has documented the general decline in survey response rates over the past decade (2013). Even some official U.S. Census Bureau surveys of the general public have response rates in the range of 10–30% (NRC, 2013). The NRC report suggests that ex-post survey weighting of the data may help to reduce risks associated with a low response rate. One of the weighting techniques they recommend and which is widely used is 'raking ratio adjustment' because it can account for multiple variables that might differ somewhat between the sample and the population. Our use of the raking approach is discussed in the section on 'Statistical analyses and results' later.

To assess whether there was any systematic bias in those that did not respond to the survey, we conducted a follow-up survey of a sample of non-respondents. We called about half of the 438 of non-respondents that had working phone numbers. The responses provide some indication that most of the non-response was due to unwillingness to answer any surveys on anything (based on both the responses to the initial questions and on the high rate of refusal to participate in even a three-question survey in this follow-up exercise), and did not suggest dislike of the National Parks. Nearly 80% of those non-respondents we did talk to indicated that they do not participate in long surveys such as our 12-page survey. Half of those responding indicated that they had visited a National Park in the past two years; and 80% of the non-respondents reached disagreed with the proposition that the U.S. government should sell off some National Parks. This suggests that assigning a zero value for National Park units and NPS programs to non-respondents when expanding our sample WTP to the population (in later sections of this chapter) yields an extremely conservative estimate of the overall value.

Survey results

Sample demographics

Most respondents answered the mailed paper questionnaire (73%), while 27% of respondents completed the survey online. The combined sample data indicates that respondents are older, more highly educated and have higher incomes than that of the entire USA. By itself, this would reduce the generalizability of the findings to the population as a whole (Figure 2.3) if no statistical corrections are made when performing the valuations. In Figure 2.3 and Table 2.2, we present the descriptive statistics for the raw survey data. The weighted sample was used in the statistical models to determine the economic values so as to be representative of the U.S. population on key characteristics that influence economic valuation.

Fifty-nine percent of survey respondents reported having visited a National Park in the past two years, whereas an independent survey regarding visitation to National Parks indicated that 47% of the American public had visited a National Park (Taylor et al., 2011). Only 8% of survey respondents indicated membership in environmental organizations.

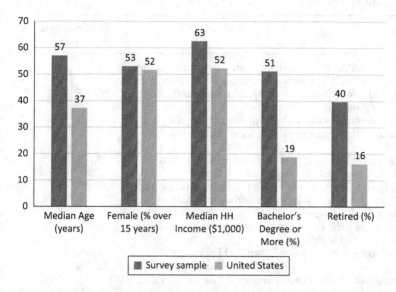

Figure 2.3 Sample and population demographics

Notes:

Sources for U.S. population data: U.S. Department of Commerce, Census Bureau, American Fact Finder (2012) and U.S. Social Security Administration.

The sample median income falls within the range $50,000 to $74,999, the number reported here is the mid-point.

Percentage retired based on 38,000,000 retirees as reported by the SSA and the U.S. population over the age of 18.

As another check on the representativeness of our sample, we compared our sample's National Park visitation to the visitation levels reported in NPS annual reports. According to those reports, the average annual number of recreation visits for 2012–2015 was 283 million. Using our survey respondents' reported visitation frequency we calculated a weighted average per household annual visitation. Applying this to the total number of households in the U.S. and using the average household size, our data implies an annual visitation of 248 million, quite close to the average number of recreation visits reported by NPS. It should be noted that this visitation metric includes all visits, rather than all visitors (i.e., it includes cases where one household made multiple visits).

Responses to attitudinal questions

Most respondents expressed support for National Parks and NPS programs, which is indicated by the responses to the Likert scale questions (Table 2.2). These were the first questions following the survey introduction and the description of the various types of National Park areas and programs.

Table 2.2 Attitudes toward the NPS units and NPS programs

Statement	% of respondents who agree [a]
1. It is important to me that historic sites are protected for current and future generations whether I visit them or not.	94.9%
2. National Park areas are good places to bring children to learn about nature.	96.2%
3. Local governments do not need any help from the National Park Service to protect local historic sites and buildings.	14.6%
4. I enjoy visiting historic sites and buildings.	89.8%
5. The U.S. should sell off some National Parks.	6.2%
6. Local governments should be able to provide trails, parks and open spaces in communities without the help of the National Park Service.	39.9%
7. I enjoy using local trails, parks and open spaces in my community and in other places.	86.6%
8. I do not benefit directly from National Parks.	14.7%
9. Private businesses could probably do a better job than the federal government at protecting local historic sites and buildings.	22.2%
10. It is important to me that trails, parks, and open spaces in communities are protected for current and future generations, whether I use them or not.	93.5%
11. National Parks are important to me because I enjoy visiting them.	80.8%
12. It is important to me that National Parks are preserved for current and future generations whether I visit them or not.	94.8%

a   Percentage of respondents indicating they either 'agree' or 'strongly agree' with the statement.

Responses to WTP valuation questions

Additional evidence of support for the National Parks and NPS programs is found in the 77–81% of respondents willing to pay some amount to prevent cuts. Eighty-one percent of respondents chose either survey Option B or Option C as their most preferred, indicating that they are willing to pay to prevent selling some or all of lands in national parks. A smaller percentage (77%) were willing to pay to prevent some or all program cuts (indicated by choosing Option E or Option F).

The WTP questions were followed by two questions that elicit respondent's views of the significance or importance of their answers in shaping policy regarding NPS parks and programs. About half of the respondents were certain that their answers to survey questions would be used to inform policy decisions about NPS parks or programs. About half the respondents were also certain they would have to pay the tax described in the survey. This last response suggests that many respondents treated their answer as potentially having real tax consequences to their household.

To identify whether refusals to pay even the lowest dollar amount were simply protests to the notion of paying higher taxes versus 'valid' WTP responses of NPS Parks or programs we asked additional questions. These questions probed whether these responses were valid (i.e., due to inability to pay even the lowest amount or low value of NPS parks or programs) or ideological aversion to paying taxes in general. Thirteen percent of respondents would not pay the lowest amount for National Parks indicated that either they could not afford the lowest amount or that National Parks or NPS programs were not worth the amount asked. Likewise, 17% of respondents would not pay the lowest amount for programs also indicated that either they could not afford the lowest amount or that NPS programs were not worth the lowest amount asked. This indicates that respondents were, in fact considering their budget constraints and their personal valuations for the National Parks or NPS programs. Such reasons for refusing to pay are *not* a protest since their refusal to pay reflects their true willingness and ability to pay.

Only about 7.5% of respondents to the National Parks choice question (58.9% of those choosing Option A) and 9.2% of respondents to the programs choice question (56% of those choosing Option D) were determined to be general 'protest' responses. This relatively low rate of protest response suggests that our 'simulated market' and scenario was accepted by more than 90% of respondents. It should be noted that *we included all WTP responses* in the following WTP analysis, even though it is acceptable to delete protests as not reflecting the respondent's true value (Mitchell and Carson, 1989). Retaining the protest households who declined to pay provides a conservative estimate of overall WTP.

Statistical analyses and results

Constructing respondent ranking of the options

The survey asked respondents to select the most preferred and least preferred among three different options for both parks and programs. This approach enables us to infer a ranking for the three options. The most preferred option alone provides only an indication of the respondents' top choice and does not contain as much information about the respondent's values as a ranking of all three options. Using the additional information in a rank-ordered logit (logistic regression) provides more efficient estimators for the coefficients. This in turn allows us to more confidently to derive incremental (marginal) values for the various attributes of the National Parks and NPS programs.

The attributes for the National Parks are the remaining acres (or sites) of each of the three types of park after any sales are made. Option A includes the sale of some land in all types of parks (in varying amounts). Option B includes smaller sales of land in some or all types. Option C has no land sales. The three options for programs are similar: one with cuts to all types, one with smaller cuts and one with no cuts. The attributes for programs are the amounts of the annual flow of outputs remaining for the four types of programs after any program cuts are made.

By using most preferred and least preferred options, the data can be configured into what is essentially a panel with each respondent having three lines of data (one for each of the three survey options). Each of these lines of data includes the attribute levels of that option (including price) and the implied rank of that option derived from the most preferred and least preferred (incomplete responses were dropped from the analysis). We then used the implicit ranking of each option as the dependent variable in a rank-ordered logit model with the attribute levels for each option as the right-hand-side explanatory variables.

Weighting to make the sample representative

As described previously, our raw sample is not completely representative for some demographic characteristics nor for the National Park visitation rate of the population as a whole. To adjust for differences between respondents' National Park visitation rates and sample demographics, we used a statistical routine to reweight the sample observations to reflect population characteristics.

Specifically, the statistical software (Stata) constructed a weight for each respondent based on their specific demographic characteristics relative to the U.S. population. The software did this by comparing the survey sample proportions with the proportions based on the most recent U.S. Census. For example, less educated, younger minorities are underrepresented in the sample, so these respondents' answers were given a larger weight than more educated, white retirees with higher incomes (who were overrepresented in the sample). National Park visitors are also overrepresented and thus were weighted less than non-visitors. We constructed three sets of weights—one based on demographic characteristics only, one based only on visitation and a third based on both demographics and visitation.

Rank-ordered logit regression analyses

We estimated several rank-ordered logit models using the weights described above to account for demographic differences and differences in visitation rates. Our TEV results are quite robust to the various weighting procedures. The results reported here are those from the best performing model. Two criteria were used in judging the best model. First, the model that provided the most statistically efficient coefficient estimates—smallest standard errors—and therefore yielded the tightest confidence intervals around WTP. Second, the model that also yielded the most conservative valuations. Since demographics are often determinants of National Park visitation (Henrickson and Johnson, 2013; Neher et al., 2013), weighting on visitation may implicitly adjust for demographics as well.

Table 2.3 Results for National Parks—rank-ordered logit—weighted for National Park visitation

Dependent variable = rank of the NPS Park policy option

	Coefficient	Std. Error	Z	P>|z|
Annual cost of option (federal income tax)	−0.0017724	0.0002924	−6.06***	0.000
Nature-focused NPS (cuts avoided)	2.49E-08	6.99E-09	3.57***	0.000
History-focused NPS (cuts avoided)	0.0068598	0.0017039	4.03***	0.000
Water-focused NPS (cuts avoided)	3.60E-07	1.14E-07	3.14***	0.002
Number of observations = 1941	Wald Chi-Sq(4) = 232.03		Log pseudo-likelihood = −1133.892	
Number of groups = 647 (3 observations per groups)	Prob > Chi-Sq = 0.0000			

*** *significant at 99% confidence level.*

The National Parks model summarized in Table 2.3 performs well over-all. Each individual coefficient is significant at the 99% confidence level and all have the expected sign. Most importantly, the coefficient on the annual cost of each option (tax) is negative and statistically significant, indicating respondents were paying close attention to the cost of each option. Put another way, the negative sign indicates that the higher the cost of that option, the less likely respondents were to choose it. Thus respondents appear to be making rational economic choices. Furthermore, the Wald statistic (distributed Chi-Square) indicates that the overall model is statistically significant.

Results for NPS programs are shown in Table 2.4. As with the parks model, the programs model performs well overall. All of the coefficients have the expected signs, and all but one (transfer of recreation lands to communities) are significant at the 95% level or higher. The Wald statistic indicates the overall model is statistically significant as well.

Estimates of economic value for National Parks and NPS programs

The implicit prices for each type of National Park and NPS program (marginal values) are estimated individually per unit (per acre, per site or per student). These marginal values are then multiplied by the number of acres, sites or students to arrive at a total value for each attribute. We then calculate TEV by summing these park- or program-specific values.

Incremental (marginal) values for the attributes are calculated as the ratio of the attribute coefficient over the price coefficient (Holmes and

Table 2.4 Results for National Park programs—rank-ordered logit—weighted for National Park visitation

Dependent variable = rank of the NPS program policy option

	Coefficient	Std. Error	Z	P>|z|
Annual cost of option (federal income tax)	–0.0041514	0.0003244	–12.8***	0.000
Historic sites and buildings protected each year (cuts avoided)	0.0006566	0.0002887	2.27**	0.023
Acres transferred to communities each year (cuts avoided)	0.0001513	0.0002011	0.75	0.452
Natural landmarks protected each year (cuts avoided)	0.012672	0.0051371	2.47**	0.014
School children served by NPS educational programs each year (cuts avoided)	6.91E-07	1.09E-07	6.33***	0.000
Number of observations = 1902	Wald chi2(5) = 244.06		Log pseudo-likelihood	
	Prob > chi2 = 0.0000		= –1117.304	
Number of groups = 634 (Three observations per groups)				

*** *significant at 99% confidence level,* ** *significant at 95% confidence level,* * *significant at 90% confidence level.*

Adamowicz, 2003). The statistical software (Stata) has a command that calculates the ratio and estimates the standard error and a confidence interval for this ratio (i.e., the incremental value). This gives us a range within which the estimated marginal and total values fall. The values implied by the rank-ordered logit regression results are shown in Table 2.5 (National Parks) and Table 2.6 (NPS programs).

The last row in Table 2.5 labeled 'All National Parks' contains two estimated values. The first is the TEV calculated using the range of acres and historic sites protected (cuts avoided) presented in the survey. The avoided cuts that households were 'buying' range from 10–40% of all National Parks. Thus the row labeled 'TEV survey cuts avoided' reflects the sample range of cuts. The resulting WTP amounts are quite reasonable, with TEV amounting to $523.86 per household, with a 95% confidence interval of $377.52 to $670.19. Unfortunately, there are few other nationwide land preservation programs with which to compare our estimates. Just to provide some perspective, Walsh et al. (1984) found Colorado households would pay on average $91.14 (in 2014 dollars) to protect 10 million acres of roadless land as Wilderness. Carson and Mitchell (1993) estimated the benefits of improving national water quality to swimmable conditions at $438 per

Table 2.5 Marginal and per-household TEVs for National Park lands, waters, and historic sites

		Estimated value	95% confidence interval for estimated value	
Nature-focused National Parks (79,096,632 acres)	Marginal value (per acre)	$0.0000141	$0.000006	$0.00002.21
	Per-household TEV for survey cuts avoided	$189.21	$83.54	$294.88
	Per-household TEV for all acres	$1,113.24	$491.51	$1,734.97
History-focused National Parks (226 sites)	Marginal value (per site)	$3.87	$1.74	$6.00
	Per-household TEV for survey cuts avoided	$148.66	$66.75	$230.57
	Per-household TEV for all sites	$874.71	$392.75	$1,356.68
Water-focused National Parks (4,818,275 acres)	Marginal value (per acre)	$0.000203	$0.00005.99	$0.000346
	Per-household TEV for survey cuts avoided	$185.99	$54.90	$317.08
	Per-household Total Economic Value for all acres	$977.93	$2,88.64	$1,667.22
All National Parks	Per-household TEV for survey cuts avoided	$523.86	$377.52	$670.19
	Per-household TEV for all acres/sites	$2,967	$2,144	$3,787

Table 2.6 Marginal and per-household values for NPS programs

		Estimated value	95% confidence interval for estimated value	
Historic sites	Marginal value (per site)	$0.16	$0.02	$0.29
and buildings protected	Per-household TEV for survey cuts avoided	$48.40	$7.47	$89.32
each year (2,000)	Per-household TEV for all sites	$316.31	$48.82	$583.80
Acres	Marginal value (per acre)	$0.04	$0	$0.13
transferred to communities	Per-household TEV for survey cuts avoided	$15.20	$0	$54.60
each year (2,700)	Per-household TEV for all acres	$98.41	$0	$353.53
Natural	Marginal value (per site)	$3.05	$0.71	$5.40
Landmarks protected	Per-household TEV for survey cuts avoided	$54.94	$12.75	$97.14
each year (114)	Per-household TEV for all sites	$347.98	$80.74	$615.22
School children served by NPS	Marginal value (per student)	$0.000167	$0.000109	$0.000224
educational programs	Per-household TEV for survey cuts avoided	$135.29	$88.73	$181.84
each year (4.1 million)	Per-household TEV for all students	$682.62	$447.70	$917.53
All programs outcomes	Per-household total value for cuts avoided	$253.82	$226.68	$280.97
	Per-household TEV for all NPS programs	**$1,445**	**$1,290**	**$1,601**

household (in 2014 dollars). Our per-household values for the cuts avoided are consistent with other nationwide environmental quality programs.

The final bolded rows of Tables 2.5 and 2.6 represent scaling up the per-acre or per-site values to the entire National Park System (Table 2.5) and all NPS programs (Table 2.6) to arrive at a comprehensive per-household total for all National Parks and NPS programs.

This scaling up assumes the values per acre are linear. This is a typical convention used in applying the marginal values or implicit prices from a choice experiment. We tested for non-linearity using a quadratic rank-ordered logit model. None of the squared terms was statistically significant, and the overall performance of both non-linear rank-ordered logit models was inferior to the models presented in Tables 2.5 and 2.6. The lack of significance of the quadratic terms suggests that marginal values may in fact be *linear over the range of our data*. However, when scaling up to all National Parks and NPS programs we go beyond the range of the cuts presented to respondents in the survey.

Figure 2.4 is a stylized version of a typical total benefits curve. This curve reflects the economic principle of diminishing marginal benefits.

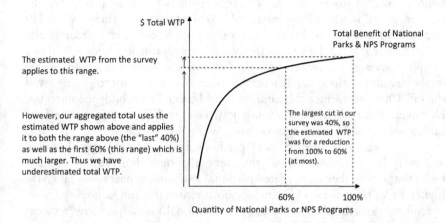

$ Total WTP

The estimated WTP from the survey applies to this range.

Total Benefit of National Parks & NPS Programs

However, our aggregated total uses the estimated WTP shown above and applies it to both the range above (the "last" 40%) as well as the first 60% (this range) which is much larger. Thus we have underestimated total WTP.

The largest cut in our survey was 40%, so the estimated WTP was for a reduction from 100% to 60% (at most).

60%   100%
Quantity of National Parks or NPS Programs

Figure 2.4 Illustration of the conservative aspect of our benefit estimates of National Parks and NPS programs

The principle states that as the quantity consumed of an identical good increases, the incremental gain in total benefits from each additional unit is a bit smaller than the benefit derived from prior units. This is easily seen when considering market goods such as additional cups of coffee, but it also applies to increasing quantity of *identical* public good (Rollins and Lyke, 1998). While even similar types of NPS units (e.g. National Seashores) are not identical to one another, we will use the logic of the total benefits curve to illustrate the conservative nature of our results.

While it would have been ideal to ask households what they would have paid to avoid selling *all* the National Park units and stopping all NPS programs, we felt this was not a credible scenario. To provide a realistic policy scenario in the survey, we proposed taking away only a portion of the National Parks and NPS programs due to budget cuts and the federal deficit. As illustrated in Figure 2.4, we took our per-household values for 20–40% reductions in National Parks, and then applied that value for the average 20% cut to all 100% of the Parks or programs.

The Parks and programs being 'bought back' by survey respondents are in the flatter portion of the TEV curve due to diminishing marginal benefit (Rollins and Lyke, 1998; Walsh et al., 1984). Thus, the WTP to avoid the cuts proposed in the survey (20–40%) would likely be lower than the WTP to avoid cuts to the remaining 60% of National Parks and NPS programs. By applying the estimated marginal value to all the units and all the program outputs we are likely underestimating the total value of the National Park System in its entirety.

Despite this downward bias in our approach, scaling our estimate of WTP to avoid an average of 20% cuts and applying it to the WTP for maintaining 100% of the entire National Park System results in a substantial figure of $2,967 per household. The equivalent WTP for all (100%) of the NPS programs is $1,445 per household. While the sum of these two WTPs is quite large, a typical household in our sample could still theoretically afford to pay it since the sum of the two figures represents about 7% of our sample's average household income. For lower-income households, some might be able to afford to pay to avoid the 20% cuts but not to pay to avoid the full 100% cuts, since this amount would exceed their budget constraint. However, it must be remembered that an average WTP means that half the sample would pay this amount or more, while the other half would pay this amount or *less*. The 'average' WTP per household does not imply that each and every household would pay the average amount. For example, households that report they have visited National Parks in the past two years have higher TEVs since their TEVs include both visitor use and non-use/passive-use value. Households that do not visit National Parks have lower values per household since their TEVs are purely non-use/passive use and do not include any current visitor-use value.

It is worth noting that the values we estimated for the National Parks are much higher than those for the NPS programs. This difference in economic values is likely due to the nature of these two public goods. The questionnaire proposed selling lands and sites within the NPS system. This would be an irreversible change. Reducing the funding for many of the NPS programs, on the other hand, is potentially reversible at some future date. It may result in some lost opportunities for historic or natural preservation but (as noted above) many of the iconic examples are protected within the park system.

Calculating national TEV of National Parks and NPS programs

To calculate the TEV of the NPS we used the estimated per-household total values for parks and programs and applied these to all U.S. households. We wanted to avoid any possibility of overstating the total value so we adjusted the values in two ways:

First, to be extremely conservative in our valuation, we assumed that those households that did not respond to the survey would not pay anything for the preservation of National Parks or NPS programs. Using our response rate of 18% we took the average per household value estimated from our sample and multiplied it by 18% of the total U.S. households (18% of 115.6 million U.S. households) and assumed zero benefits for the remaining 82% of households. This clearly understates the total value, since many households may simply choose not to answer lengthy surveys such as ours even though they still place some value on National Parks and NPS programs.

Second, we attributed a zero value to all those who did not return the survey form—even though there are many reasons why people do not participate in any surveys, especially long ones such as ours. We used a conservative method for weighting responses and for estimating respondents' economic values. In every step of the methodology we erred heavily on the conservative side.

Using this procedure our conservative estimated TEV is $92 billion, of which $62 billion is for National Parks and $30 billion for NPS programs, which often exist outside the geographical boundaries of NPS units. The $62 billion can be disaggregated by groups of NPS units with $23.3 billion for nature-focused NPS units, $18.3 billion for history-focused NPS units, and $20.4 billion for water-based NPS units. The $30 billion for NPS programs can also be disaggregated with $6.6 billion for history programs, $2 billion for NPS-facilitated transfer of lands to communities for recreation, $7.2 billion for protection of natural landmarks of significance to local communities and $14.2 billion for NPS programs aimed at school children.

We conclude that the estimated value of $62 billion for National Parks is credible given that Neher et al. (2013) estimated the recreation-use value for the National Parks at $28.5 billion. It makes sense that TEV—which includes recreation use values and passive or non-use values—would be significantly larger. If we subtract the Neher et al. estimate from our TEV for National Parks, it yields an estimate of $33.5 billion for the purely passive or non-use value, i.e., the existence and bequest value derived by the American public from just knowing that National Parks exist and will be available for future generations.

We believe our $92 billion valuation represents the minimum amount that U.S. households are willing to pay to avoid the loss of the NPS and its programs. We selected a highly conservative methodology and used conservative assumptions in conducting the survey:

- Attributing value to only the 18% of households who responded to the survey and attributing zero value to the remaining 82%. (Our follow-up non-response check confirmed that most non-respondents failed to respond due to factors that were unrelated to the national parks, and indeed they are overwhelmingly favorable to national parks.)
- Using WTP to keep National Park lands/waters/historic sites instead of the more appropriate WTA to give up these places that people already own. WTA is usually much larger than WTP for public goods.
- Not dropping 'protest responses'—people who indicated they would not pay either for reasons such as rejecting one or more premises of the survey, sometimes called 'scenario rejection' or being ideologically opposed to taxes.
- Valuing only a 20–40% reduction in National Park lands/waters and historic sites, but assumed that same value per acre or per site applied to loss of all National Park lands/waters and historic sites. This is akin to estimating that a person would value the loss of five fingers at five times the value of losing one finger, when in fact a person would pay more to avoid the loss of all five fingers.

- Selecting the economic valuation model that gave us the lowest estimate of what households would pay.
- Excluding questions on the value of additional NPS activities, such as scientific research, ecosystem services and other sources of value.

Our values are also in line with WTP estimates from other nationwide CVM surveys regarding environmental programs. Carson and Mitchell (1993: 2452) estimated a value of improving America's rivers and lakes to a swimmable water quality at $29.2 billion in 1983, equivalent to $69.5 billion in 2015 dollars. This estimate is similar in magnitude to our estimate of the value of National Park lands, waters, and historic sites. A CVM study of the national benefits of maintaining air quality over just three southwest U.S. National Parks (Grand Canyon, Mesa Verde, and Zion) was estimated by Schulze et al. (1983: 166) at $6.1 billion in 1980, with inflation-adjusted benefits of $17.8 billion in 2015. Given, that the Schulze et al. value is just for maintaining air quality over these three National Parks, not transferring them to the private sector, suggests our estimates for maintaining the entire National Park System lands, waters, and historic sites are quite reasonable.

Conclusion

Our results indicate that the American public's value for the non-market public goods produced by the NPS is substantial. The lands, waters, historic sites, and programs of the National Park System are worth $92 billion—at a minimum.

Of the $62 billion that is related just to the lands of National Park System, less than half represents the value of recreational use. The remainder is the value that American households place on *just knowing* that lands, waters, and historic sites of the National Park System exist and will be available for future generations.

The NPS's programs aimed at conservation, education, and stewardship of historic and cultural sites are valued by the American public at $30 billion. These programs benefit millions of Americans who visit protected properties as well as large numbers of teachers and students who use educational curricula materials developed by NPS. But this figure may well underestimate the value that the public places on the NPS role in protecting ecosystems, watersheds, intellectual property, and other assets that were not specifically tested in this survey.

Despite these limitations, we are confident that our estimates represent a minimum economic value for NPS assets and programs. By including only the value of the NPS to U.S. households, our estimates omit completely the economic value of the NPS to hundreds of millions of people worldwide, a significant number of whom come as tourists to visit the National Parks, or who value the existence of these places. Moreover, the findings are supported by a number of recent opinion polls that provide evidence of strong support for public lands in general (National Forest Foundation 2013 poll http://www.nationalforests.org/poll) and the National Parks in particular (National Parks Conservation Association poll 2012 http://www.npca.org/protecting-our-parks/policy-legislation/national-parks-poll.html).

Importantly, the methodology outlined in this chapter should be of interest both to analysts and to policymakers who are considering the appropriate level of budgetary resources needed to maintain a significant state park asset in their own state or national park system in their own country.

Chapter Acknowledgments

This study benefited from survey design and review of statistical analysis provided by Dr. Barbara Kanninen of BK Econometrics, and initial study design and draft report review by Dr. John Duffield, University of Montana. We are grateful for the assistance of Dr. Brian Harnisch at Wyoming Survey and Analysis Center, University of Wyoming, Laramie, WY. Additional input was gratefully received from Dr. Dan McCollum and Dr. Tom Holmes of the USDA Forest Service and Brian Quay, now an economist with the Center for Disease Control.

We also acknowledge the contributions of former students Francis Choi and Timothy Marlowe at the Harvard Kennedy School.

We benefitted from the input and assistance of a number of individuals in the NPS, including former Director Jonathan Jarvis and his Senior Advisor Loran Fraser. Dr. Bruce Peacock, an economist at NPS, provided NPS with his vision of the principles that such a valuation study should follow. Dr. Lynne Koontz and Dr. Leslie Richardson provided valuable comments on the draft report.

We are grateful for the funding for this research, which has been provided by the S. D. Bechtel, Jr. Foundation, the Turner Foundation, Cody J. Smith (Summit Foundation), the National Park Foundation, and UPD Consulting. We especially thank Tina Batt and Cody J. Smith for bringing this study to fruition.

Finally, Dr. Sandra Gudmundsen's careful attention to detail while editing this chapter has greatly improved its clarity and readability.

None of these funding groups or individuals is responsible for the content of this chapter and its conclusions, which are solely the authors'.

References

Arrow, K., R. Solow, P. Portney, E. Leamer, R. Radner, and H. Schuman. 1993. Report of the NOAA Panel on Continent Valuation. http://www.economia.unimib.it/DATA/moduli/7_6067/materiale/noaa%20report.pdf (Also published in Federal Register January 15, 1993, 4601–4614.)

Bennett, J. and R. Blamey. 2001. *The Choice Modelling Approach to Environmental Valuation*. Cheltenham, UK: Edward Elgar Publishing Ltd. 269 pp.

Berrens, R. P., A. K. Bohara, H. C. Jenkins-Smith, C. L. Silva, and D. L. Weimer. 2004. Information and effort in contingent valuation surveys: application to global climate change using national internet samples. *Journal of Environmental Economics and Management* 47: 331–363.

Boyle, K. J. and M. A. Markowski. 2003. Estimating Non-Use Values for National Park System Resources. White paper obtained from authors.

Carlsson, R., P. Frykblom, and C. J. Lagerkvist. 2005. Using cheap talk as a test of validity in choice experiments. *Economics Letters* 89(2): 147–152.

Carson, R. and R. C. Mitchell. 1993. The value of clean water: the public's willingness to pay for boatable, fishable and swimmable quality water. *Water Resources Research* 29(7): 2445–2454.

Carson, R. T. and T. Groves. 2007. Incentive and informational properties of preference questions. *Environmental and Resource Economics* 37: 181–201.

Champ, P. A., K. J. Boyle, and T. C. Brown. 2003. *A Primer on Nonmarket Valuation*. Norwell, MA: Kluwer Academic Publishers. 576 pp.

Choi, F. and T. Marlow. 2012. The Value of America's Greatest Idea: Framework for Total Economic Valuation of National Park Service Operations and Assets and Joshua Tree National Park Total Economic Value Case Study. A report provided to the NPS, developed for the Policy Analysis Exercise Requirement at the Harvard Kennedy School of Government. 87 pp.

Cummings, R. G. and L. O. Taylor. 1999. Unbiased value estimates for environmental goods: a cheap talk design for the contingent valuation method. *American Economic Review* 89(3): 649–665.

Duffield, J. W. 2006. Economic Values of National Park System Resources Within the Colorado River Watershed. Report prepared for the National Park Service Environmental Quality Division, Cooperative Agreement H1200040002, Task J2380050112. 47 pp.

Evans, J. R. and A. Mathur. 2005. The value of online surveys. *Internet Research* 15(2): 195–210.

Freeman, A. M. 2003. *The Measurement of Environmental and Resource Values: Theory and Methods*, Second Edition. Washington, DC: Resources for the Future. 491 pp.

Grandjean, B. D., N. M. Nelson, and P. A. Taylor. 2009. Comparing an internet panel survey to mail and phone surveys on willingness to pay for environmental quality: A national mode test. Paper Presented at the 64th Annual conference of the American Association for Public Opinion Research, 14–17 May 2009. 5779–5793.

Hanemann, M. 1991. Willingness to pay and willingness to accept: How much can they differ? *American Economic Review* 81(3): 635–647.

Henrickson, K. and E. Johnson. 2013. The demand for spatially complementary national parks. *Land Economics* 89(2): 330–345.

Hensher, D. A., J. M. Rose and W. H. Greene. 2005. *Applied Choice Analysis: A Primer*. Cambridge, UK: Cambridge University Press. 717 pp.

Holmes, T. P. and W. L. Adamowicz. 2003. Attribute based methods. In *A Primer on Nonmarket Valuation*. Champ, P. A., K. J. Boyle, and T. C. Brown (Eds.). Dordrecht/Boston/London: Kluwer Academic Publishers. pp. 171–219.

Horowitz, J. and K. McConnell. 2002. A review of WTA/WTP studies. *Journal of Environmental Economics and Management* 44(3): 426–447.

Horowitz, J. and K. McConnell. 2003. Willingness to accept, willingness to pay and the income effect. *Journal of Economic Behavior and Organization* 51: 537–545.

Kaplowitz, M. D., T. D. Hadlock, and R. Levine. 2004. A comparison of web and mail survey response rates. *Public Opinion Quarterly* 68(1): 94–101.

Krutilla, J. V. 1967. Conservation reconsidered. *American Economic Review* 57(4): 777–786.

Leggett, C. G., N. S. Kleckner, K. J. Boyle, J. W. Duffield, and R. C. Mitchell. 2003. Social desirability bias in contingent valuation surveys administered through in-person interviews. *Land Economics* 79(4): 561–575.

Lindhjem, H. and S. Navrud. 2011. Using internet in stated preference surveys: a review and comparison of survey modes. *International Review of Environmental and Resource Economics* 5: 309–351.

Louviere, J. J., D. A. Hensher, and J. D. Swait. 2000. *Stated Choice Methods: Analysis and Application*. Cambridge, UK: Cambridge University Press. 402 pp.

Mitchell, R. C. and R. T. Carson. 1989. *Using Surveys to Value Public Good: The Contingent Valuation Method*. Washington, DC: Resources For the Future. 463 pp.

NPS. n.d. *National Park Service Programs: A Companion Volume to NPS Management Policies*. Washington, DC: National Park Service.

National Research Council. 2013. *Nonresponse in Social Science Surveys*. Washington, DC: National Academy Press.

Neher, C., J. Duffield, and D. Patterson. 2013. Valuation of National Park System visitation: the efficient use of count data models, meta-analysis, and secondary visitor survey data. *Environmental Management* 52(3): 683–698.

Orme, B. 2010. *Getting Started with Conjoint Analysis*, Second Edition. Research Publishers, LLC: Madison, WI. https://www.sawtoothsoftware.com/download/techpap/samplesz.pdf.

Poole, B. D. and D. K. Loomis. 2010. A comparative analysis of mail and internet surveys. In *Proceedings of the 2009 Northeastern Recreation Research Symposium*. Gen. Tech. Rep. NRS-P-66. Watts, Clifton E. Jr. and Fisher, Cherie LeBlanc (eds.). Newtown Square, PA: U.S. Department of Agriculture, Forest Service, Northern Research Station. pp. 231–234.

Rollins, K. and A. Lyke. 1998. The case for diminishing marginal existence values. *Journal of Environmental Economics and Management* 36: 324–344.

Schulze, W. D., D. S. Brookshire, E. G. Walther, K. K. MacFarland, M. A. Thayer, R. L. Whitworth. S. Ben-David, W. Malm, and J. Molenar. 1983. The economic benefits of preserving visibility in the National Parklands of the Southwest. *Natural Resources Journal* 23: 149–173.

Schulze, W. D., D. S. Brookshire, E. G. Walther, K. Kelley, M. A. Thayer, R. L. Whitworth, S. Ben-David, W. Maim, and J. Molenar. 1985. The benefits of preserving visibility in the National Parklands of the Southwest. In *Methods Development for Environmental Control Benefits Assessment*, Volume VIII. EPA-230-12-85-026. 21 pp.

Silva, A., R. M. Nayga, B. L. Campbell, and J. L. Park. 2011. Revisiting cheap talk with new evidence from a field experiment. *Journal of Agricultural and Resource Economics* 36(2): 280–291.

Stratus Consulting. 2015. *Economic Evaluation of Restoration Actions for Salmon and Forests and Associated Wildlife in and Along the Elwha River*. Boulder, CO: Stratus Consulting .

Taylor, P. A., B. D. Grandjean, and J. Gramann. 2011. National Park Service Comprehensive Survey of the American Public. Natural Resources Report NPS/

NRSS/SSD/NRR—2011/432. Laramie, WY: Wyoming Survey and Analysis Center, University of Wyoming.

Taylor, P. A., N. M. Nelson, B. D. Grandjean, B. Annatchkova, and D. Aadland. 2009. Mode Effects and other Potential Biases in Panel-Based Internet Surveys: Final Report. Prepared for National Center for Environmental Economics, Office of Policy, Economics, and Innovation, U.S. Environmental Protection Agency, Washington, DC. WYSAC Technical Report No. SRC-905. Laramie, WY: Wyoming Survey & Analysis Center, University of Wyoming. 60 pp.

Turner, R. W. 2012. Using Contingent Choice Surveys to Inform National Park Management. Paper presented at the Association for Environmental Studies and Sciences Conference. June 21–24, 2012, Santa Clara, California. 45 pp.

U.S. Environmental Protection Agency. 2010. *Guidelines for Preparing Economic Analyses.* Washington, DC: Environmental Protection Agency. 300 pp.

U.S. Office of Management and Budget. 1992. Circular No. A-94 Revised. Memorandum for Heads of Executive Departments and Establishments, Guidelines and Discount Rates for Benefit-Cost Analysis of Federal Programs. https://www.whitehouse.gov/omb/circulars_a094/.

U.S. Water Resources Council. 1983. *Economic and Environmental Principles and Guidelines for Water and Related Land Resources Implementation Studies.* 137 pp.

Vossler, C. A. and M. F. Evans. 2009. Bridging the gap between the field and the lab: environmental goods, policy maker input, and consequentiality. *Journal of Environmental Economics and Management* 58(3): 338–345.

Walsh, R., J. Loomis, and R. Gillman. 1984. Valuing option, existence and bequest demands for wilderness. *Land Economics* 60(1): 14–29.

Welsh, M. P., R. C. Bishop, M. L. Phillips, and R. M. Baumgartner. 1997. Glen Canyon Dam. Colorado River Storage Project, Arizona: Nonuse Values Study, Final Report. Prepared for U.S. Department of the Interior, Bureau of Reclamation, Upper Colorado Regional Office, Salt Lake City UT Report No. EC-97-10. 382 pp.

Wyoming Survey and Analysis Center. 2013. *Cost Proposal: Your National Park Service Lands and Programs.* Laramie, WY: University of Wyoming.

3 Estimating visitor use and economic contributions of National Park visitor spending

Lynne Koontz and Catherine Cullinane Thomas

Introduction

National Parks not only protect and preserve the places we most value, but they also are significant economic engines in nearby communities across the nation. Different ways National Parks support economic activity include: spending by National Park Service (NPS) visitors in communities near parks; local purchases of supplies and services for park operations; employee payroll spending in nearby communities and beyond; grants and payments to communities from NPS programs; and restoration and construction activity from NPS infrastructure repair investments. This category of economic benefits has traditionally been reported for visitor spending on an annual systemwide basis by the NPS. Strictly speaking, economists categorize these impacts as regional economic contributions rather than benefits.

Lands managed by the NPS are part of a diverse system of natural, cultural and historic landscapes, representing 28 different designations, including National Parks, monuments, battlefields, historic sites, lakeshores, seashores, recreation areas, and scenic rivers and trails, in urban, rural, and sometimes remote settings. Visitors arrive and travel through parks in a variety of ways including cars, buses, cruise ships, bicycles, canoes, on horseback, and on foot. Each NPS site is unique; the method of assessing visitors and their spending patterns must be customized to the site while providing consistent metrics across the park system. This chapter provides an overview of the NPS methods for estimating visitor spending and calculating economic contributions of visitor spending in terms of jobs supported, wage and labor income, and total economic activity.

Overview of visitor spending contributions

Visitors to National Parks incur travel expenditures for items such as hotels, camping, food, tours, local transportation, and souvenirs. This spending directly supports local businesses in these tourism-related sectors. Because businesses purchase goods and services from one another, an increase in the final demand for a good or service can generate a ripple effect throughout an economy affecting downstream industries. This is called the multiplier effect. In the case of visitor spending, NPS visitors buy goods and services from regional businesses and vendors, generating *direct* effects within the economy. To meet this demand, local businesses purchase inputs to produce these goods and services, and input suppliers purchase additional inputs from other industries, thus creating a ripple of *indirect* effects within the economy. Additionally, employees of all these businesses use their incomes to purchase household goods and services, generating further *induced* effects of visitor spending. The sum of the indirect and induced effects gives the *secondary* effects of visitor spending, and the sum of the direct and secondary effects gives the total economic effect of visitor spending in an economy.

Economic input-output models capture these interactions between producers and consumers as regional economic multipliers; multipliers capture the size of the secondary effects, usually as a ratio of total effects to direct effects (Leontief, 1986). Impacts are generated only by money spent within a specified geographic region; expenditures that happen outside of the region are considered 'leakages' from the model. Therefore, the size of the region included in an input-output model influences the magnitude of economic multipliers. As the geographic area considered as the economic region expands, there are fewer leakages because more suppliers are included in the multiplier effect. Figure 3.1 illustrates how NPS visitor spending supports jobs and business activity in local economies.

Economic contributions measure the total economic activity within a regional economy stemming from visitor spending, and include the effects of spending by both local visitors who live within gateway regions and non-local visitors who travel to NPS sites from outside of gateway regions. An economic contributions analysis should not be confused with an economic impact analysis. Economic impact analyses are like economic contribution analyses, but estimate the net changes to the economic base of a regional economy that can be attributed to the inflow of new money to the economy from non-local visitors (i.e., economic impact analyses exclude spending made by local visitors because it is assumed that local visitors would likely still spend their money in the local area whether or not they visit the park). Economic impacts can be interpreted as the economic activity that would likely be lost from the local economy if the National Park was not there.

The NPS first started measuring and reporting the economic contributions of visitor spending with the development of the Money Generation Model (MGM) in 1990 (NPS, 1995). An updated version of the Money Generation Model (MGM2) was used to produce the first systemwide estimates of economic contributions in 2001 (Stynes & Sun, 2003). Starting in 2005, NPS systemwide estimates have been published on an annual basis. In 2012, the MGM2 model was replaced by the Visitor Spending Effects (VSE) model. The VSE model builds on the framework developed by Stynes et al. (2000) for the MGM2 while increasing the ability to update and improve input data over time (Cullinane Thomas, Huber, & Koontz, 2014). The Stynes

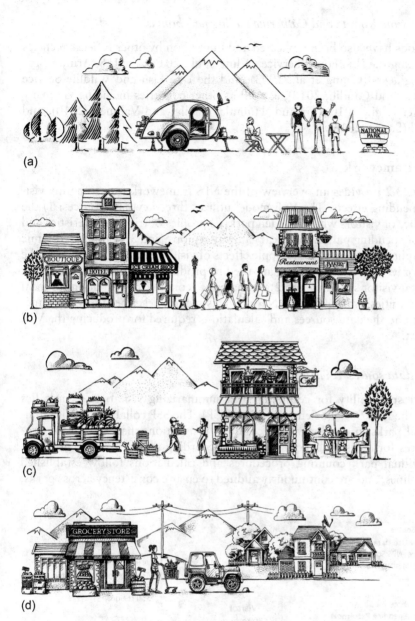

Figure 3.1 NPS visitor spending supports jobs and business activity in local economies. (a) Over 300 million visitors travel to NPS sites across the US every year. (b) These visitors spend money in local communities; the sales, income and jobs resulting from these purchases represent the *direct* effects of visitor spending. (c) Additional jobs and economic activity are supported when businesses purchase supplies and services from other local businesses, thus creating *indirect* effects of visitor spending. (d) Employees use their income to purchase goods and services in the local economy, generating further *induced* effects of visitor spending

Source: Cullinane Thomas, Koontz, and Cornachione (2018).

methods have also been replicated and built upon by other Federal agencies including the U.S. Forest Service (White et al., 2013), the U.S. Army Corps of Engineers (Chang et al., 2003), and the U.S. Fish and Wildlife Service (Carver and Caudill, 2013), as well as other countries including Germany (Mayer et al., 2010), Finland (Huhtala, Kajala, and Vatanen, 2010), and Brazil (Souza, 2016).

VSE framework

Figure 3.2 provides an overview of the NPS framework for estimating visitor spending effects. The VSE model utilizes three key data sources: 1) the number of visitors who visit each park; 2) profiles of trip characteristics and visitor spending patterns in local gateway regions; and 3) regional economic multipliers that describe the ripple effects of visitor spending throughout the economy. These data sources are used to produce two results: 1) estimates of total visitor spending and 2) estimates of economic contributions to local communities, states, and the Nation. This section describes the VSE framework and the data sources and calculations required for producing the VSE results.

VSE data source 1: visitor use data

The responsibility for compiling and summarizing visitation records lies with the NPS Social Science Program (SSP). The SSP collaborates with individual parks to develop visitor counting instructions that contain the procedures for measuring, compiling, and recording required visitor use data. Individual park counting procedures and calculations follow established guidelines, and are continuously audited to ensure consistency across parks,

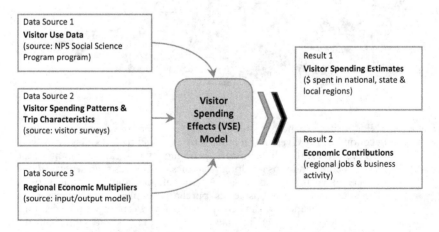

Figure 3.2 VSE framework

to maintain the integrity of the data, and to ensure that the data and calculations are statistically sound (see Ziesler and Pettebone, 2018; Ziesler and Singh, 2018 for full details). Consistency among parks is maintained by implementing count systems that conform to a standard set of use definitions. The basic unit of measurement is a 'visit', which is the entry of a person onto lands or waters administered by the NPS. The applicable rule is that NPS counts one entrance per individual per day as a visit. For example, a family of four taking a week-long vacation to Yellowstone National Park and staying at a lodge outside of the park would be counted as 28 visits (four individuals who enter the park on seven different days). A different family of four, also taking a week-long vacation to Yellowstone National Park but stays at a lodge within the park, would be counted as four visits (four individuals who enter the park on a single day and then stay within the park for the remainder of their trip). These differences are a result of the limitations in the methods available to count park visits.

The NPS currently collects monthly recreation visit counts for 382 of the 419 National Park Service units (NPS units). Other parks are unable to report visitor use for a variety of reasons (e.g., the park is too new to be open for regular, scheduled visitation, or the park is administered by another agency). The SSP analyzes and publishes official visitation statistics on a monthly basis, and produces annual summaries at the end of each calendar year. The results are easily accessible on the NPS visitor use statistics website (irma.nps.gov/stats), and are used to support a variety of internal and external analyses related to park visitation.

VSE data source 2: visitor spending profiles

Visitor surveys are used to collect the essential visitor spending and trip characteristic data necessary for developing spending profiles to represent distinct visitor spending patterns for each park. Visitor spending profiles for the VSE model are derived from survey data collected through the NPS Visitor Services Project (VSP). These surveys measure visitor characteristics and visitor evaluations of importance and quality for services and facilities.

VSP surveys follow established best practice guidelines for collecting visitor spending data, which include sampling travel parties, eliciting total party expenditures, and using mail-back surveys to gather data on each party's total spending within the local area for the full duration of their trip (Stynes and White, 2006). A party is defined as a group that is traveling together and sharing expenses (e.g., a family). Respondents are asked to report their party's expenditures during their time inside the park and local areas within 60 miles surrounding the park. Expenditure categories include spending on lodging (hotels, motels, and bed and breakfasts), camping fees, restaurants, groceries, fuel, local transportation, guides and tour fees, equipment rental, souvenirs, clothing, supplies, and other retail. Also included are purchases within the NPS unit such as guide and tour fees, retail, and lodging to capture economic contributions related to concessionaire operations.

Respondents who live outside of the surrounding park area are not asked to report expenses that occurred at home or en-route to the local impact area. Respondents residing within the surrounding park area are asked to report only expenditures that were directly related to their park visit.

For the development of visitor spending profiles, best practice guidelines suggest estimating separate spending profiles for subgroups of visitors with distinct spending patterns (Stynes and White, 2006). White and Stynes (2008) found that segmenting by trip type explains more of the variation in recreation visitor spending patterns than other strategies such as segmenting by recreation activity. The VSE model first segments visitors by six lodging-based trip types including: local day trips, non-local day trips, overnight stays in lodging within the park, overnight stays in lodging outside of the park, overnight camping within the park, and overnight camping outside of the park. A seventh segment, 'other', describes the spending patterns of visitors staying overnight in private homes, with friends or relatives, or in another unpaid lodging.

Visitor spending profiles are estimated for visitors on day trips as spending per party per day or (for visitors on overnight trips) as spending per party per night. Total party days/nights are defined as the sum of the number of days (for day trips) or the number of nights (for overnight trips) that parties spend visiting a park. To estimate total party-days/nights, park visit data from the SSP program are combined with trip characteristic information derived from the VSP surveys. The trip characteristic data required to make these conversions are average party size, entry rates (i.e., the average number of days parties enter the park over the course of a trip), and length of stay (i.e., the average number of days that parties spend visiting the park). (See Cullinane Thomas, Koontz, and Cornachione, 2018 for full details).

VSE data source 3: regional economic multipliers

The VSE model utilizes multipliers specifically developed for the geographic area surrounding each park. Geographic information systems (GIS) data were used to determine the local gateway region for each park unit by spatially identifying all counties partially or completely contained within a 60-mile radius around each park boundary. As an exception, the economic regions for parks in Alaska and Hawaii are defined as the State of Alaska and the State of Hawaii because of the state-level interconnectedness of tourism travel within these states. Multipliers are derived from the IMPLAN software and data system, a commercially available and widely used input-output modeling system available in the United States[1]. Four types of regional economic contributions are estimated:

- **Jobs** measures the annualized full and part-time jobs supported by NPS visitor spending.

- **Labor income** measures the employee wages, salaries and payroll benefits, as well as the incomes of sole proprietors that are supported by NPS visitor spending.
- **Value added** measures the contribution of NPS visitor spending to the Gross Domestic Product of a regional economy. Value added is equal to the difference between the amount an industry sells a product for and the production cost of the product. Value added includes labor income, interest, profits, and indirect businesses taxes.
- **Economic output** measures the total estimated value of the production of goods and services supported by NPS visitor spending. Economic output is equal to value added plus intermediate expenditures.

The VSE analysis reports economic contributions at the park-level, state-level, NPS administrative region-level, and national level. Park-level contributions use county-level IMPLAN models comprised of all counties contained within the local gateway regions; state-level contributions use state-level IMPLAN models; NPS regional-level contributions use regional IMPLAN models comprised of all states contained with the NPS administrative region; and the national-level contributions use a national IMPLAN model. Because the size of the region included in an IMPLAN model influences the leakages out of the region and the magnitude of the economic multiplier effects, economic contributions at the national level are larger than the sums of those at the regional level, the state level, and the individual National Park unit level.

VSE result 1: total visitor spending

The VSE model combines visitor spending patterns and trip characteristic data with visitor use data to estimate total visitor spending. As shown in Figure 3.3, steps to estimate visitor spending include: separating visitors into distinct visitor segments that describe differences in spending patterns; transforming visitor count data and visitor spending profiles into comparable units of measure; and determining the portion of the time that visitors spend in local gateway economies that can be attributed to their National Park visit.

Table 3.1 shows NPS systemwide visitor spending estimates by visitor segments for 2017.

VSE result 2: economic contributions of visitor spending

Economic contributions of visitor spending to local economies are estimated by multiplying total visitor spending by regional economic multipliers. Direct spending for each of the defined spending categories—lodging (hotels, motels, and bed and breakfasts), camping fees, restaurants, groceries, fuel, local transportation, recreation industries (admission fees, and guide fees),

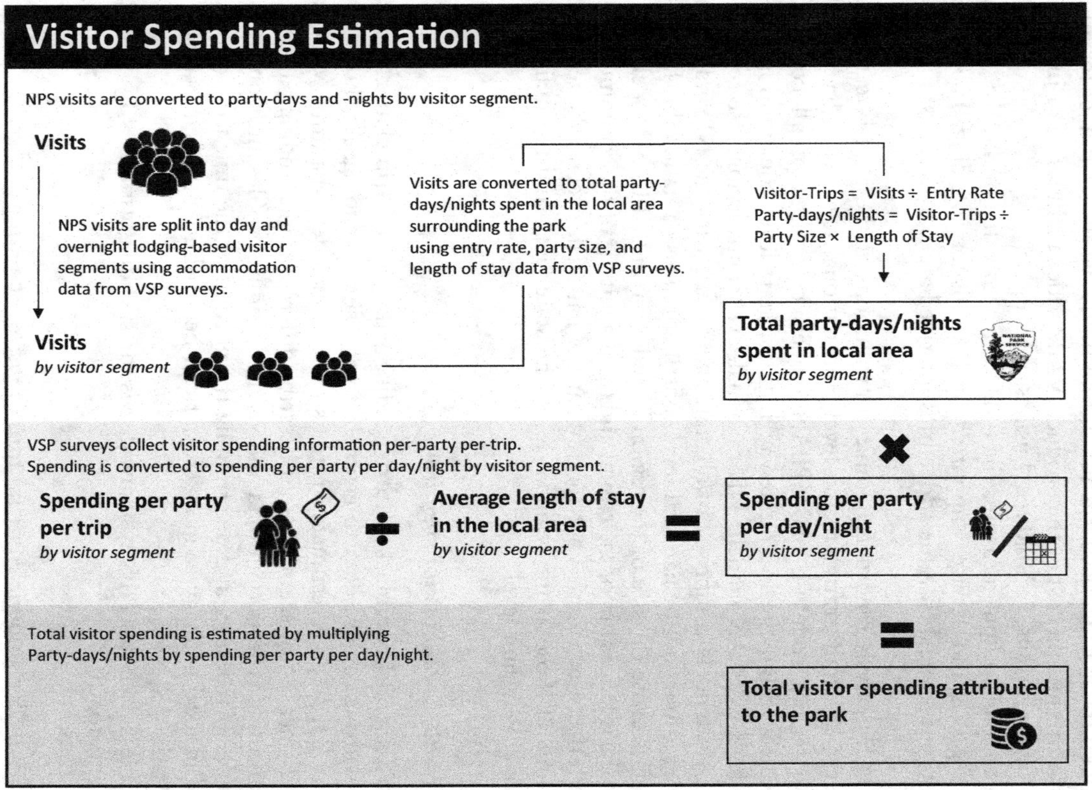

Visitor Spending Estimation

Visits

NPS visits are converted to party-days and -nights by visitor segment.

NPS visits are split into day and overnight lodging-based visitor segments using accommodation data from VSP surveys.

Visits
by visitor segment

Visits are converted to total party-days/nights spent in the local area surrounding the park using entry rate, party size, and length of stay data from VSP surveys.

Visitor-Trips = Visits ÷ Entry Rate
Party-days/nights = Visitor-Trips ÷ Party Size × Length of Stay

Total party-days/nights spent in local area
by visitor segment

×

VSP surveys collect visitor spending information per-party per-trip. Spending is converted to spending per party per day/night by visitor segment.

Spending per party per trip
by visitor segment

÷

Average length of stay in the local area
by visitor segment

=

Spending per party per day/night
by visitor segment

=

Total visitor spending is estimated by multiplying Party-days/nights by spending per party per day/night.

Total visitor spending attributed to the park

Figure 3.3 Process for estimating visitor spending

Table 3.1 Visitor spending estimates by visitor segment for 2017

Visitor segment	Total spending ($ millions, 2017-$)	Percent of total spending	Average spending per party per day/ night (2017-$)	Average number of people per party
Local day trip	$1,062.2	5.8%	$41.72	2.9
Non-local day trip	$2,908.9	16.0%	$90.00	3.0
NPS lodge	$453.6	2.5%	$421.28	3.2
NPS camp ground	$434.3	2.4%	$124.86	3.3
Motel outside park	$11,274.7	62.0%	$284.44	2.8
Camp outside park	$1,094.7	6.0%	$126.51	3.3
Other	$953.7	5.2%	$42.14	3.2
Total	$18,182.1	100%	$136.44	3.0

Source: Cullinane Thomas, Koontz, and Cornachione (2018).

and souvenirs—are mapped to corresponding sectors of the economy, and IMPLAN multipliers are calculated for each spending category. The VSE model inflates all dollar values to the analysis year, aggregates park-level visitor spending estimates to state and national totals, and multiplies visitor-spending estimates by park, state, and national-level economic multipliers (Cullinane Thomas, Koontz, and Cornachione, 2018). Table 3.2 shows the national-level contribution estimates for 2017.

To increase the utility of the VSE annual report results, the NPS collaborated with the U.S. Geological Survey to develop a web-based interactive data visualization tool. This interactive tool is available at https://www.nps.gov/subjects/socialscience/vse.htm. The top half of Figure 3.4 illustrates how users can view the current year's visitor spending, jobs, labor income, value added, and economic output by sector for 1) all parks in the national economy, 2) all parks located in a particular state economy, or 3) individual park economies (e.g., the economy surrounding an individual park). The lower half of Figure 3.4 provides year-by-year trend data for the geographic region selected (in Figure 3.4, the data shown are for the national economy).

VSE data limitations

Accurate estimation of visitor spending effects requires high-quality survey data representative of the variety of visitor uses and demographics seen across the park system. Only 57 of the 419 NPS parks have conducted visitor surveys that include visitor spending questions. Increased sampling rigor across all park types and geographic regions would increase the accuracy of

Table 3.2 NPS visitor spending economic contributions to the national economy for 2017

Effects	Sector	Jobs	Labor income ($ millions, 2017-$)	Value added ($ millions, 2017-$)	Output ($ millions, 2017-$)
Direct effects	Hotels, motels, and B&Bs	49,064	$1,834.1	$3,592.7	$5,531.5
	Camping and other accommodations	8,503	$265.1	$294.2	$445.7
	Restaurants and bars	60,447	$1,351.2	$2,075.2	$3,697.7
	Grocery and convenience stores	5,255	$167.3	$246.3	$360.0
	Gas stations	4,148	$156.0	$178.1	$274.8
	Transit and ground transportation services	8,583	$369.5	$865.7	$1,364.1
	Other amusement and recreation industries	29,378	$674.2	$1,028.2	$1,812.3
	Retail establishments	21,173	$495.8	$566.5	$874.2
Total direct effects		186,551	$5,313.2	$8,846.9	$14,360.3
Secondary effects		119,686	$6,618.8	$11,428.4	$21,390.6
Total effects		306,237	$11,932.0	$20,275.0	$35,751.0

Source: Cullinane Thomas, Koontz, and Cornachione (2018).

Economic Contributions to the National Economy

In 2017, 331 million park visitors spent an estimated $18.2 billion in local gateway regions while visiting National Park Service lands across the country. These expenditures supported a total of 306 thousand jobs, $11.9 billion in labor income, $20.3 billion in value added, and $35.8 billion in economic output in the national economy.

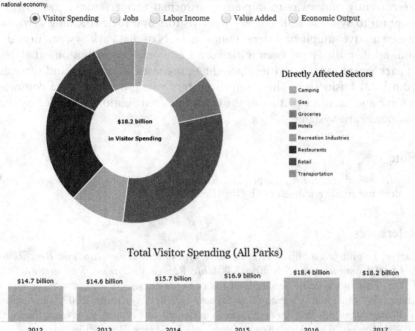

Figure 3.4 VSE web-based interactive data visualization tool (https://www.nps.gov/subjects/socialscience/vse.htm)

park-specific trip characteristic and spending data, and improve the accuracy of future visitor spending effects analyses.

To address this issue, the NPS is in the process of establishing a formal socioeconomic monitoring (SEM) program that will provide a standard visitor survey instrument, and a long-term, systematic sampling design for in-park visitor surveys. The NPS recently completed pilot SEM visitor surveys in 16 parks. Full implementation of the SEM program will result in a greater number of parks having primary survey data updated regularly, and the SEM sampling design will ensure that sampled parks are statistically representative of the system. In addition to improving sampling rigor, the new SEM survey instrument provides the opportunity to modify and add additional visitor spending related questions to the original VSP survey questions. These new questions will help address limitations with the currently available VSP data, and will enable the exploration of improved visitor spending estimation methodologies.

Conclusions

Over the past 25 years, the NPS has successfully developed methods and tools to estimate visitor spending effects for a diverse range of parks. Efforts are currently underway to implement a formal socioeconomic monitoring program to systematically survey park visitors and their spending across a representative sample of different units in the National Park System. In addition, pilot studies have been initiated for expanded contributions analyses of park operational activities, including purchases of supplies and services from local businesses. These improvements will provide a more comprehensive and accurate picture of the economic contributions provided by the National Park System.

Note

1 Any use of trade, firm, or product names is for descriptive purposes only and does not imply endorsement by the US Government.

References

Carver, E. and J. Caudill. 2013. *Banking on Nature—The Economic Benefits to Local Communities of National Wildlife Refuge Visitation.* Washington, DC: U.S. Fish and Wildlife Service Division of Economics.

Chang, W. H., D. B. Propst, D. J. Stynes, and R. S. Jackson. 2003. *Recreation Visitor Spending Profiles and Economic Benefit to Corps of Engineers Projects.* Washington, DC: U.S. Army Corps of Engineers Recreation Management Support System.

Cullinane Thomas, C., C. Huber, and L. Koontz. 2014. 2012 National Park Visitor Spending Effects—Economic Contributions to Local Communities, States, and the Nation. Natural Resource Report NPS/NRSS/EQD/NRR—2014/765. Fort Collins, CO: National Park Service.

Cullinane Thomas, C., L. Koontz, and E. Cornachione. 2018. 2017 National Park Visitor Spending Effects—Economic Contributions to Local Communities, States, and the Nation. Natural Resource Report NPS/NRSS/EQD/NRR—2018/1616. Fort Collins, CO: NPS. https://www.nps.gov/subjects/socialscience/vse.htm.

Huhtala, M., L. Kajala , and E. Vatanen. 2010. Local Economic Impacts of National Park Visitors' Spending in Finland: The Development Process of an Estimation Method. Working Papers of the Finnish Forest Research Institute. Vantaa, Finland: Metla. Retrieved 31 July 2017 from http://www.metla.fi/julkaisut/workingpapers/2010/mwp149.pdf.

Leontief, W. 1986. *Input-Output Economics*, Second Edition. New York: Oxford University Press.

Mayer, M., M. Müller, M. Woltering, J. Arnegger, and H. Job. 2010. The economic impact of tourism in six German National Parks. *Landscape and Urban Planning* 97(2): 73–82.

National Park Service. 1995. *The Money Generation Model.* Denver, CO: National Park Service.

Souza, Thiago Do Val Simardi Beraldo. 2016. Recreation Classification, Tourism Demand and Economic Impact Analyses of the Federal Protected Areas of Brazil. A Dissertation Presented to the Graduate School of the University of Florida in Partial Fulfilment of the Requirements for the Degree of Doctor of Philosophy.

Stynes, D. J., D. B. Propst, W. Chang, and Y. Sun. 2000. *Estimating National Park Visitor Spending and Economic Impacts: The MGM2 Model.* East Lansing, MI: Michigan State University.

Stynes, D. J. and Y.-Y. Sun. 2003. *Economic Impacts of National Park Visitor Spending on Gateway Communities: Systemwide Estimates for 2001.* East Lansing, MI: Michigan State University.

Stynes, D. J. and E. M. White. 2006. Reflections on measuring recreation and travel spending. *Journal of Travel Research* 45(1): 8–16.

White, E. M., D. B. Goodding, and D. J. Stynes. 2013. Estimation of National Forest Visitor Spending Averages from National Visitor Use Monitoring: Round 2. PNW-GTR-883. Portland, OR: US Department of Agriculture, Forest Service, Pacific Northwest Research Station.

White, E. M. and D. J. Stynes. 2008. National forest visitor spending averages and the influence of trip-type and recreation activity. *Journal of Forestry* 106(1): 17–24.

Ziesler, P. and D. Pettebone. 2018. Counting on visitors: a review of methods and applications for the National Park Service's visitor use statistics program. *Journal of Park and Recreation Administration* 36: 39–55.

Ziesler, P. and P. Singh. 2018. Statistical abstract: 2017. Natural Resource Data Series NPS/NRSS/EQD/NRDS—2018/1156. Fort Collins, Colorado: National Park Service.

4   Valuing carbon sequestration in the U.S. National Parks

Current conditions and future trends

Adam Banasiak, John B. Loomis, and Linda J. Bilmes

Overview

This chapter estimates current and future sequestration of carbon on lands within U.S. National Park Service units (hereafter NPS units) in the continental USA. We demonstrate a methodology that can be applied to other protected areas in the USA as well. Specifically, using land cover data and associated carbon sequestration rates during a five-year baseline period, this chapter calculates the current tonnage and economic value of vegetative carbon sequestration services on all NPS units located in the continental USA. Average projected sequestration amounts for the period 2006–2050 are also provided based on modeled data. Using conservative assumptions, we find that current average annual carbon sequestration on NPS units' land amounts to 17.5 million metric tons of CO_2, valued at $752.5 million dollars using the Federal interagency working group social cost of carbon damage price of $43/metric ton (updated to 2018 dollars). In the future years through 2050, absent any changes in land management (such as invasive species removal or fire management) carbon sequestration is predicted to fall by 31% to an average of 12.0 million metric tons of CO_2 sequestered annually, due to factors such as a warming climate and increased fire hazards.

Introduction

While protected natural areas deliver many ecosystem services that have economic values, carbon sequestration is one that has not previously been quantified for the NPS units as a whole. In a demonstration of the general approach for quantifying and valuing carbon on U.S. Fish and Wildlife Service National Wildlife Refuges, Patton et al. (2015) quantified the economic value of carbon sequestration at four Refuges. This chapter presents the first economic analysis of vegetative carbon sequestration services provided by lands within NPS units, both at present and projected to 2050. Our analysis is organized by ecosystem region and ecosystem type (e.g., forest, wetland, grassland) to emphasize the broad applicability of these services across a wide range of protected ecosystems inside and outside of the NPS units.

Methodology

The general method used in this study looks at each NPS unit individually, then in the aggregate. At each NPS unit, we apply a formula to determine the annual flow of carbon from atmospheric to terrestrial reservoirs:

$$\text{Net ecosystem carbon balance rate}_{ij} * \text{NPLarea}_{ij} = \text{volume of carbon}_{ij}$$

Where i is vegetation type, i=1,2,3; j is ecoregion, j=1...15; NPLarea is the amount of NPS unit land with vegetation i in ecoregion j.

As a first step we estimated the total annual amount of carbon sequestration based on historic data using the following series of calculations:

1 We determined the total forest, grassland, and wetland acreage in each NPS unit (excluding other land cover types such as ice and developed areas).
2 We then looked at the location of each NPS unit to determine what ecoregion it is in. We determined the relevant net ecosystem carbon balances (NECBs) rate for each ecosystem and ecoregion—how much carbon on average an acre of forest, grassland, or wetland vegetation in that ecoregion transfers from the atmosphere to terrestrial storage per calendar year.
3 We multiplied the total area of forests, wetlands, and grassland in each NPS unit by the appropriate carbon sequestration rate for the ecoregion, and summed carbon sequestered in the three vegetation types to get the grand total tonnage of sequestered carbon for the NPS unit.
4 We repeated the process for each NPS unit. The sum of the totals creates the estimated tonnage of carbon sequestration in the National Park Service (NPS).
5 We then applied an economic damage per ton of carbon as explained in more detail below.

Data sources

Our methodology requires four types of information:

- Land areas within NPS unit boundaries.
- Ecosystem types and areas within those boundaries and an identification of the ecoregion for each NPS unit.
- The average amount of carbon sequestered for each ecosystem in each ecoregion.
- Damage cost per ton of carbon dioxide emitted.

The relevant sources for this data are as follows:

a   NPS unit boundaries. NPS unit types and boundaries are provided in several formats (including for ArcGIS) by the NPS online at: http://map services.nps.gov/arcgis/rest/services/LandResourcesDivisionTractA ndBoundaryService/MapServer.

b   Ecosystem areas. The 2011 National Land Cover Database (NLCD) was used to determine the area of different ecosystems within each NPS unit. This dataset is assembled by the Multi-Resolution Land Characteristics Consortium (MRLC, 2011). The consortium's goal of providing consistent national coverage of land use data in the public domain (i.e., free and readily downloadable) is ideal for this application. Data is coded into 16 land cover classes (12 vegetation classes and four developed classes). The dataset is updated every five years. Ecosystem types were aggregated into three classes: forests, grasslands, and wetlands. These vegetated areas account for over 85% of the total land area of NPS acreage in the continental USA based on an analysis of the 2011 NLCD data. All other land cover types, such as developed and agricultural areas, were excluded from further analysis. Since the lands in question are administered by the NPS, the share of developed and agricultural lands is minimal (typically <5%) for larger parks. Areas categorized as open water, barren, or perennial snow/ice were also excluded because no national peer-reviewed dataset of carbon sequestration rates for such areas is available. However barren areas can sequester carbon through a series of reactions between minerals and acidic rainwater. Aquatic life, such as corals and foraminifera, also plays a large role in the global carbon cycle. Therefore, the exclusion of these areas makes our estimate conservative.

c   Net ecosystem carbon balances. Plants cycle carbon back and forth through the atmosphere as they grow, die, and decompose, are burned in fires and grow again. The net of all these activities is the measure of carbon sequestration: how much carbon is added to or subtracted from the atmosphere once all vegetative processes are accounted for? This parameter, known as the "net ecosystem carbon balance" (NECB), captures the rate, or flow, at which carbon is exported from the atmosphere and into storage in the living vegetative layer (biosphere) where it can rest for hundreds of years or for even longer in the pedosphere (soil layer) of the Earth. The NECB is influenced by both how much carbon plants can store in a year and also by how much is released by disturbances and decay. Climatic variables such as rainfall and temperature exert the most direct influence on vegetative growth. Ecosystem age and health are also important. While age structure and health vary across NPS units, applying a single NECB is not an issue for our investigation because we have a sufficiently large enough sample size—millions of acres for most ecoregions—where we can assume ecosystem age and health approximate a normal distribution. While some individual acres are sequestering more and some less, applying the median to all acres is a reasonable approximation. However, other land managers, if they wish to use our method to estimate their carbon sequestration values, should keep this consideration in mind.

d Region, ecosystem, and climate-specific net NECBs are available from USGS LandCarbon National Assessment Program (https://www2.u sgs.gov/climate_landuse/land_carbon/), a Congressionally-mandated assessment. The USGS LandCarbon NECBs are based on historical data for the period 2001–2005 using variables such as fire frequency and severity, rainfall, and temperature data as model inputs, as well as incorporating data used for detailed models conducted on forest growth and sequestration by other agencies, such as the U.S. Forest Service.

Since the climate of the United States is so varied, the LandCarbon National Assessment divides the continental USA into 15 regions. These correspond to the EPA Level II ecoregion boundaries. Ecoregions are defined by both biotic and abiotic factors, such as climate, soils, and vegetation assemblages[1]. For each ecoregion, LandCarbon provides the NECB for several different types of land cover, including forest, grassland/shrublands, wetlands, and agricultural use.

Baseline NECBs are calculated using three different models (a spreadsheet model, an erosion-deposition carbon model (EDCM), and the CENTURY model) linked to a General Ensemble Biogeochemical Modeling System (GEMS). The models are run for each year of the baseline period (see Zhu, 2010 for more details). The minimum and maximum output of each model was reported for the Western Region, while the minimum, average, and maximum outputs were reported for the Eastern Region[2]. For the Great Plains ecoregion, only the average was reported[3].

LandCarbon compares its data and NECB estimates to both measured and computed NECBs from other studies to assess the accuracy of the model output. Where data is available, intermediate products are also compared to existing measured and calculated data, for example the USDA's forest biomass estimates[4].

e Estimated future NECBs. In addition to the baseline estimates for current conditions, NECB estimates for the period 2006–2050 are also available. Since the future is uncertain, LandCarbon performed 21 GEMS model runs under varying scenarios. As with the baseline calculations, LandCarbon used the Spreadsheet, EDCM, and CENTURY models, this time in conjunction with three different future climate assumptions taken from the UNEP IPCC-SRES[5]. LandCarbon calculated the projected NECBs as the difference between the carbon stocks in adjacent years. The annual projected NECBs for the period 2006–2050 were then averaged for each model run. The result is the total average NECB for the entire period 2006–2050 rather than any specific year. For the Eastern U.S. Region, the minimum, average, and maximum NECBs resulting from these 21 models are reported. For the Western region, only the minimum and maximum results are reported. For the Great Plains ecoregion, only the average is reported.

Carbon sequestration results

Baseline assessment

Using the baseline carbon sequestration rates from the period 2001–2005 and the method outlined in the preceding, we calculated the present-day annual carbon sequestration value for the NPS units in the continental USA (CONUS). The average annual amount of carbon sequestered into terrestrial sources is estimated to be nearly 17.5 million metric tons of carbon dioxide. Nearly one-fifth (18.6%) of the total sequestration in all NPS units occurs in Everglades National Park and adjacent Big Cypress National Preserve. Outside of the NPS context, Table 4.1 demonstrates that measurable positive carbon sequestration occurs in all ecoregions across the USA, with significant contributions coming from all three major ecosystems types investigated (forests, grasslands, and wetlands). This suggests the broad applicability of measuring this ecosystem service to protected lands across the USA, regardless of the type of ecosystem protected.

A simple per-acre carbon storage analysis of this data (final column of Table 4.1) reveals an important insight regarding the distribution of carbon sequestration and geographic distribution of NPS units. The highest carbon sequestration ecosystems within the NPS system are in the eastern half of the USA, as are all top five highest-ranked ecoregions. Both of the top-ranked ecosystems are also non-forests. On the other hand, most of the NPS unit acreage is in the Western United States. Thus policy analysts looking primarily for carbon sequestration based climate solutions should consider emphasizing eastern regions for land protection. Likewise, Congressional representatives and the NPS officials in eastern regions considering possible new protected areas in these regions should consider this additional national benefit of carbon sequestration in their decisions.

There is a wide range—a more than seven-fold difference—between the maximum and the minimum national estimates shown in Table 4.1. Unfortunately, the LandCarbon data source does not provide confidence intervals for its NECB data. This is because some of the model inputs do not have well-bounded error ranges and because the models used to generate the output are not fully integrated. Rather, LandCarbon chose to use a selection of models to generate the greatest likely range, in its professional opinion, of potential outcomes.

Nonetheless, this estimate of NPS carbon sequestration services should be viewed as conservative. This study excludes non-vegetative carbon

Table 4.1 Baseline and projected vegetative carbon sequestration in continental U.S. NPS lands broken out by ecoregion and ecosystem

Ecoregion	Baseline (2001–2005) tons CO₂			Future (2006–2050) Tons CO₂			Total m²	Base avg. (tons CO₂/ m²) x 10,000
	Min	Average	Max	Min	Average	Max		
Atlantic Highlands	44,145	74,677	84,294	7,168	66,286	93,118	156,082,500	5
Forest	43,333	68,540	77,886	6,356	63,850	90,141	119,690,100	6
Grassland	0	4,513	4,513	0	0	0	3,766,500	12
Wetland	812	1,624	1,895	812	2,436	2,977	3,781,800	4
Central USA Plains	196	252	-398	-932	185	308	4,906,800	1
Forest	196	252	280	31	185	308	604,800	4
Grassland	0	0	-678	-963	0	0	2,172,600	0
Wetland	0	0	0	0	0	0	0	0
Cold Desert	-343,783	774,449	1,892,680	-128,962	581,989	1,292,940	18,975,357,000	0
Forest	-163,531	343,416	850,363	87,197	463,234	839,271	2,889,449,100	1
Grassland	-180,251	405,566	991,383	-216,159	100,874	417,908	10,409,622,300	0
Wetland	0	25,467	50,935	0	17,881	35,762	107,310,600	2
Mississippi Alluvial & SE Coastal Plains	1,000,045	3,593,994	5,295,135	784,396	3,491,129	5,068,814	8,073,393,300	4
Forest	34,640	231,819	357,055	-43,465	189,382	336,851	371,340,900	6
Grassland	0	27,137	45,228	-6,437	9,655	19,311	235,363,500	1
Wetland	965,406	3,335,038	4,892,852	834,297	3,292,092	4,712,652	6,987,053,700	5
Marine West	246,789	793,347	1,339,904	-356,682	702,003	1,760,688	4,197,224,700	2
Forest	246,789	692,909	1,139,028	-356,682	624,194	1,605,070	3,344,652,000	2
Grassland	0	100,438	200,876	0	59,968	119,936	355,473,000	3
Wetland	0	0	0	0	17,841	35,682	55,956,600	0
Mediterranean California	62,857	340,694	618,532	26,063	229,675	433,286	1,757,076,300	2

(Continued)

Table 4.1 Continued

Ecoregion	Baseline (2001–2005) tons CO_2			Future (2006–2050) Tons CO_2			Total m^2	Base avg. (tons CO_2/ m^2) x 10,000
	Min	Average	Max	Min	Average	Max		
Forest	89,127	149,116	209,105	68,823	134,206	199,588	279,954,900	5
Grassland	-18,844	191,578	402,000	-42,760	85,521	213,802	1,272,707,100	2
Wetland	-7,426	0	7,426	0	9,948	19,896	18,431,100	0
Mixed Wood Plains	**201,223**	**300,880**	**338,743**	**872**	**285,382**	**464,809**	**947,039,400**	**3**
Forest	161,795	250,483	270,857	-14,213	232,583	383,762	483,695,100	5
Grassland	12,003	12,003	24,006	0	0	13,163	73,557,900	2
Wetland	27,425	38,395	43,879	15,085	52,799	67,884	120,823,200	3
Mixed Wood Shield	**259,855**	**552,982**	**697,244**	**-98,330**	**530,071**	**886,729**	**2,244,015,900**	**2**
Forest	208,257	429,808	549,445	-171,653	338,667	649,498	1,336,022,100	3
Grassland	11,690	17,535	23,380	0	5,805	5,805	60,510,600	3
Wetland	39,908	105,639	124,419	73,323	185,599	231,426	367,085,700	3
Ozark-Ouachita-Appalachian	**1,381,415**	**2,607,931**	**3,513,578**	**271,572**	**1,901,878**	**3,202,883**	**4,909,306,500**	**5**
Forest	1,376,412	2,566,942	3,452,095	266,717	1,871,696	3,167,846	4,492,696,500	6
Grassland	0	20,976	31,464	0	10,761	10,761	111,640,500	2
Wetland	5,003	20,013	30,019	4,855	19,421	24,276	35,368,200	6
Great Plains	**58,803**	**191,111**	**291,077**	**259,819**	**259,819**	**259,819**	**2,666,650,500**	**1**
Forest	7,729	25,119	38,258	161,426	161,426	161,426	230,510,700	1
Grassland	45,327	147,312	224,367	65,901	65,901	65,901	1,342,022,400	1
Wetland	5,748	18,681	28,452	32,492	32,492	32,492	170,148,600	1
SE Plains	**391,921**	**1,001,081**	**1,489,785**	**21,911**	**743,647**	**1,340,500**	**1,778,049,000**	**6**
Forest	299,718	742,538	1,126,528	-69,828	483,621	1,010,345	1,254,352,500	6
Grassland	-2,503	15,015	25,025	-2,716	8,148	19,012	111,473,100	1
Wetland	94,705	243,527	338,232	94,454	251,878	311,143	328,934,700	7

(Continued)

Table 4.1 Continued

Ecoregion	Baseline (2001–2005) tons CO_2			Future (2006–2050) Tons CO_2			Total m^2	Base avg. (tons CO_2/ m^2) x 10,000
	Min	Average	Max	Min	Average	Max		
Warm Desert	-882,444	2,051,003	4,984,449	-1,601,692	-51,993	1,497,706	36,174,987,000	1
Forest	-93,666	93,666	280,999	0	117,650	235,301	1,032,543,000	1
Grassland	-788,777	1,957,336	4,703,450	-1,601,692	-222,457	1,156,777	32,139,887,400	1
Wetland	0	0	0	0	52,814	105,628	92,760,300	0
Western Cordillera	1,818,661	5,217,196	8,615,731	607,820	3,309,449	6,011,077	28,428,523,200	2
Forest	1,807,720	4,145,766	6,483,813	646,811	2,739,706	4,832,601	13,747,384,800	3
Grassland	-25,692	924,898	1,875,488	-38,991	493,883	1,026,758	9,735,044,400	1
Wetland	36,633	146,532	256,430	0	75,859	151,719	365,263,200	4
Grand total	4,239,685	17,499,597	29,160,754	-206,979	12,049,518	22,312,678	110,312,612,100	2

sequestration that is occurring in the marine areas of the NPS, such as in the coral reefs. Additionally, in the realm of vegetated areas, we have limited our analysis of areas classified by the 2011 NLCD to forest, wetland, or grassland/shrubland. This excludes some areas, such as dune vegetation and sparsely vegetated desert areas as well as some fields and grasslands, which may be listed as agricultural. However, these are generally relatively small areas in terms of acreage of NPS units.

Nationwide assessment: looking into the future

As a second step, we estimated the future NPS carbon sequestration (Table 4.1). We utilized the same methodology as for the baseline estimate reported above, except this time using the predicted average carbon sequestration rates for the period 2006–2050. To keep the two estimates comparable, we kept the same restrictions and classification scheme of NPS units as the baseline. One important methodological point to note, however, is that the future estimates show the average annual NECB for the period 2006–2050, not just the NECB for the year 2050. This makes the attribution of economic values much more difficult because most estimates of the economic damages avoided by carbon sequestration increase non-linearly with time. While in theory this same effect is occurring for the baseline period 2001–2005, the time period is so much shorter that the practical effect of this issue is negligible in the baseline time period. Given the difficulty of estimating an average carbon value over the 2006–2050 time frame, dollar values presented in the next section have not been applied to the future predictions. Instead, we provide just the future estimated *tonnage* as a basis for comparison to 2001–2005.

Predicted future carbon sequestration rates (NECBs) are generally lower than baseline rates because the climate is expected to warm and to become more variable in the future, placing increased stress on vegetation from both hotter temperatures and less predictable precipitation. Such stresses will translate into lower vegetative growth rates because vegetation has adapted to its current environment and cannot in general adapt easily or quickly to different temperature and water regimes[6]. Drier, hotter summers also increase the potential for wildfires. In addition to releasing large amounts of carbon back into the atmosphere during the actual fire, changes in fire frequency can lower the long-term carbon sequestration rate because very young forests often have lower NECBs than middle-aged and mature forests. Our best estimate is that these variables will produce an average loss of 0.2 metric tons per acre of carbon sequestration rate averaged over all NPS unit acres in this study, in the period through 2050.

Heterogeneity in carbon sequestration outcomes from climate change across ecoregions and ecosystem types is apparent in Table 4.1. For example, the loss of capacity is spread evenly across most regions except for the Mississippi Alluvial & SE Southeast Coastal Plains region, where sequestration remains more or less unchanged. Large losses occur in the Warm Deserts, which are the only ecoregion to become a net emitter based on future (2006–2050) average predictions. Additional water and heat stress in an already marginal environment may be the cause of this reversal. This variability points to the needs to quantify and understand the potential impacts climate change can have on ecosystem service benefits. This understanding is needed so that management agencies can understand the risks posed to their protected areas and take appropriate action where possible, such as managing invasive species and decreasing fire risk. This variability suggests both risks and opportunities for land managers across the USA, and further emphasizes the need for all managers to consider carbons sequestration values in their resource management decisions. For example, managers in regions with stable values may seek to capitalize on regional stability and monetize these streams as stable marketable carbon values or offsets in order to generate funds to invest in the protection of other at-risk natural assets.

There are several key assumptions built into future NECBs. First is that the climate is warming along the trendlines identified by the UN Intergovernmental Panel on Climate Change, and consequently is the incidence of destructive fires on NPS units will increase. Second is that there will be no fundamental changes to NPS ecosystem management in response to these environmental changes. Of course, it is likely that NPS will adopt new approaches to respond to these threats. However, based on the NECB assumptions, the total sequestration on NPS units in the CONUS from 2006 to 2050 is predicted to be on average just over 12.0 million metric tons of carbon dioxide, about a 30% drop in sequestration capacity over the 2001–2005 baseline estimates. The potential future loss of carbon sequestration capacity points to the need for NPS managers to monitor vegetation and associated carbon sequestration. With this information, NPS can make informed decisions on whether to modify current management practices to slow losses in carbon sequestration in NPS units or allow ecosystems to settle into a new equilibrium.

Social damage cost of carbon (SCC)

Literature on SCC

In order to estimate the benefits of the carbon sequestrated in lands of the NPS units we used the SCC in the atmosphere. There has been a tremendous amount of research on the many economic damages from future climate change. These damages include flooding from sea level rise, increased diseases (e.g., malaria—Tol, 2005), public health issues from increased heat, water supply disruptions (due to less snow, more rain, and hotter temperatures), and a host of adverse effects on non-marketed natural resources such as increased endangerment of species to native forest dieback. Tol (2005) provides a summary of the 103 studies that attempted to provide a comprehensive estimate of the 'total' damages that a ton of carbon contributes to climate change. He found the range of damages per ton from $14 to $165 (upper 90% confidence interval) with a mean estimate of $93 per ton. The wide range of estimates is due in part to the original authors' different models, temperature increase used, differences in assumptions and models for adaptation costs, the impact of changes on the developing world, future technological change, and perhaps most importantly different rates of discounting of future benefits and costs. When Tol narrowed the sample to only include peer-reviewed literature and examined the cases using a rate time preference[7] of 3% (~social discount rate of 4–5%), the range of damages per ton shrunk, with a mean of $16 ($21 in 2018 dollars) with a 95% confidence interval upper value of $82 (2018 dollars). This finding highlighted Tol's conclusion that the largest values reported in the literature tended to use the weakest methods and most extreme assumptions.

The U.S. Federal government drew upon the same literature reviewed by Tol (2005) to arrive at a range of dollar damages for a ton of carbon at different discount rates. We use the 2013 update of the Executive Order 12866 Interagency Working Group estimate of the Social Cost of Carbon (Interagency Working Group on Social Cost of Carbon, 2013), which determined a price of per metric ton of carbon of $33 in 2010 and $38 in 2015 (both in 2007 dollars). Updating the mid-point of this range ($35.50) to 2018 dollars, yields $43 per metric ton. This estimate uses a 3% rate of discount of future consumption relative to current consumption. We recognize that there is considerable disagreement on the proper discount rate for SCC estimates, in part because of the very long time horizons involved and because of intergenerational equity concerns. Weisbach and Sunstein (2009) provide an excellent summary of the thinking behind the various approaches to the discount rate, a topic that is beyond the scope of this chapter. From a global perspective, the U.S. estimate for the social cost of carbon is somewhat lower than other national estimates found in the literature. To span the range of likely SCC and reflect the uncertainty in SCC estimates, we use the interagency median SCC associated with a 3% discount rate, Tol's peer-reviewed mean and Tol's upper 95% confidence interval.

Results of application of economic values to current carbon sequestration

Baseline volumes of sequestered carbon from Table 4.1 are converted into economic values in Table 4.2, using the three SCC estimates discussed. In the average volume case from Table 4.1 and using the Interagency SCC estimate ($43), we calculate $752.5 million in annual social benefits from carbon sequestration in the NPS units. Obviously, given the range of potential SCC values, the estimate for the economic value of the ecosystem

Table 4.2 Valuation of aggregate carbon sequestration on continental U.S. NPS lands

	Continental total for NPS avg. baseline (tons metric CO₂)	SCC (2018 $)		
		(Tol 2005) peer-reviewed 3% discount rate mean value	*Interagency Working Group 3% discount rate*	*(Tol 2005) peer-reviewed 3% discount rate (95% upper value)*
		($21)	*($43)*	*($82)*
Forest	9.75M*	$ 205	$ 419	$ 800
Grassland	3.82M	$ 80	$ 164	$ 313
Wetland	3.93M	$ 83	$ 169	$ 322
All ecosystems	17.5M	$ 368	$ 753	$ 1,435

* M = millions.

service also varies greatly, even restricting to one volume estimate. Despite the combined uncertainties in estimating the quantity of carbon sequestrated and the SCC, our estimate of $752.5 million is similar to the only other estimate of the value of carbon sequestration in NPS units found in an internal NPS report by Richardson et al. (2014) of $582 million per year. Thus, regardless of the particular details of the method used to quantify and value carbon sequestration we are fairly confident that the value of sequestration in NPS units lies in the range of $600 million–$750 million annually.

An important insight from this analysis is the order-of-magnitude for this single ecosystem service, is in the hundreds of millions of dollars. For comparison, the Federal budget appropriation by the NPS specifically designated purely for 'resource stewardship' in 2014 was only $329 million. Thus, the budget for resource stewardship is less than half of just this one value of ecosystem services provided by carbon sequestration ($753 million). The relative scale underscores the importance of incorporating the value of ecosystem services such as carbon sequestration when considering the creation of, budgeting for, and management of protected natural areas.

Estimates of the cost to the NPS of management actions to reduce future losses of carbon sequestration are not available, and estimating such costs would be a major research project itself. Therefore, we cannot calculate net benefits (benefits minus cost) to the NPS from additional management actions to maintain its current carbon sequestration. Inevitably, additional restoration activities to maintain existing carbon sequestration would enhance multiple ecosystem services (such as water storage, water filtration, or storm resilience) in addition to carbon sequestration. Other managers seeking to use our methodology should remember that carbon sequestration is only a starting point for considering the wider benefits of ecosystem services when making future management decisions on their lands.

Conclusion

While there is significant uncertainty surrounding our estimates, this study is significant in several respects both within and beyond the NPS. First, the methodology used to estimate the social benefits of the carbon sequestered in the lands of the NPS units and can be applied to any sufficiently large area in the USA. This method provides a reasonably expedient and inexpensive way for land managers to quantify the carbon sequestration provided from the natural areas they administer, e.g., wilderness areas, wildlife management areas.

Second, the order-of-magnitude of the estimate shows this ecosystem service value is significant. For example, from our estimate, the value of carbon sequestered on lands of the NPS units has a value of $752.5 million annually. The benefits of just this one single ecosystem service return about 30% of the total NPS budget of $2.5 billion to the American public.

Third, our results suggest that in future climate scenarios the amount of carbon sequestered in NPS units lands in CONUS will decline by about 30% without a substantial NPS management effort. Given the likely magnitude of the economic losses to future generations from this reduction in carbon sequestration, there may very well be justification for NPS managers to slow this loss. Further analysis is needed to make this determination, which will no doubt have to be made on an NPS unit basis. But there is a need to quickly determine if maintaining current carbon sequestration capacity is warranted, as otherwise it may be more costly to recover this capacity once it is lost.

Finally, as an example of ecosystem services, the benefits of carbon sequestration are felt around the nation and the globe. As such valuation of ecosystem services can be a useful tool to connect with new constituencies living far from NPS units and engage them in recognizing the value of better management of NPS units, other protected areas of the federal government as well as those protected acres managed by state, local, and private hands.

Notes

1 The ecoregion framework used here is derived from work by James Omernik for the U.S. EPA. The regions are the Atlantic Highlands, Central USA Plains, Cold Deserts, Mississippi Alluvial and SE Coastal Plains, Marine West Cost Forest, Mediterranean California, Mixed Wood Plains, Mixed Wood Shield, Ozark, Ouachita-Appalachian Forest, Great Plains, Southeastern USA Plains, Warm Deserts, and Western Cordillera.

2 To address this data gap for the Western Region, this paper uses the mathematical average between the reported maximum and minimum scenarios for the Western Region. We compared the Eastern Region's reported average with the mathematical average and noted that the reported average was higher than the mathematical average, suggesting this approach was conservative.

3 Since there are few NPS units in this ecoregion and this data will have only minor impact on the nationwide tally, to allow us to make nationwide minimum and

maximum assessments for all NPS units, this study uses the reported average NECBs for the Great Plains ecoregion as the minimum and maximum NECB as well.

4 The r-squared and other statistical variables comparing the results for areas where other studies have been conducted are available in the full USGS LandCarbon reports.

5 United Nations Environment Programme Intergovernmental Panel on Climate Change Special Report on Emissions Scenarios. The UNEP homepage is available at: http://www.unep.org/. A detailed description of this process can be found in the LandCarbon reports, both in the Methodology paper and starting on page 111 of the Western Region report.

6 For example, cacti have evolved a special photosynthesis pathway that allows them to open pores in their leaves and surfaces only at night for gas exchange, reducing evaporative water loss to the atmosphere and allowing them to thrive in dry environments. Such metabolic mechanisms are not available to many plants that have evolved in climates with abundant water, leaving them unprepared for periods of increased drought.

7 Time preference refers to the how much more society prefers consumption today to consumption in the future. This is often represented by a percentage interest rate, at which society trades off a dollar of benefits today for a dollar of benefits in the future. In this context, the interest rate is referred to as a 'discount rate' as it represents the amount people discount benefits received in the future compared to benefits received today.

References

Interagency Working Group on Social Cost of Carbon, U.S. Government. 2013. Technical Update of the Social Cost of Carbon for Regulatory Impact Analysis. Washington, DC. Retrieved 30 January 2019 from https://obamawhitehouse.archives.gov/sites/default/files/omb/assets/inforeg/technical-update-social-cost-of-carbon-for-regulator-impact-analysis.pdf.

Multi-Resolution Land Characteristics Consortium (MRLC). 2011. National Land Cover Database. National Land Cover Database 2011, 2014. http://www.mrlc.gov/nlcd2011.php.

Patton, D., J. Bergstrom, R. Moore, and A. Covich. 2015. Economic value of carbon storage in U.S. National Wildlife Refuge wetland ecosystems. *Ecosystem Services* 16: 94–104.

Richardson, L., C. Huber, Z. Zhu, and L. Koontz. 2014. Terrestrial Carbon Sequestration in National Parks: Values for Conterminous United States. Natural Resource Report NPS/NRSS/EQD/NRR—2014/880. Fort Collins, CO: NPS, 36 pp.

Tol, R. 2005. The marginal damage costs of carbon dioxide emissions: An assessment of the uncertainties. *Energy Policy* 33(16): 2064–2074.

Weisbach, D. and C. Sunstein. 2009. Climate change and discounting the future: A guide for the perplexed. *Yale Law & Policy Review* 27(2): 433–457.

Zhiliang Zhu, Z. (Ed.). 2010. A Method for Assessing Carbon Stocks, Carbon Sequestration, and Greenhouse-Gas Fluxes in Ecosystems of the United States Under Present Conditions and Future Scenarios. U.S. Geological Survey, Report 2010-5233. Reston, VA. http://pubs.usgs.gov/sir/2010/5233/pdf/sir2010-5233-Main.pdf.

5 Economic benefits provided by National Park Service educational resources

Tim Marlowe, Linda J. Bilmes, and John B. Loomis

Introduction

The educational role of the National Park Service (NPS) stems from its dual mission to not only preserve the USA's natural and cultural resources unimpaired, but also to provide programming, services and infrastructure that 'extend the benefits of natural and cultural resource conservation and outdoor recreation throughout this country and the world' (NPS, 2016). Through a combination of park programs and publicly available educational materials, the NPS reaches tens of millions of people every year. This includes millions of children and adults who engage in place-based educational programs as well as an even larger public that is able to access NPS materials through websites and original online content.

The education provided to children and adults by the NPS is valuable not only because it provides experiential learning but also because much of it is unique. This education is unique in that the National Park Service units (NPS units) provide the ability for students to interact directly with natural, historic, and cultural sites. This interaction deepens students' understanding of America's historic, geographic and cultural heritage. NPS focuses on place-based education (Washburn, 2013), a field that integrates student academic and developmental learning into the context of natural, socio-cultural, and historic local environments (Lieberman and Hoody, 1998).

This chapter presents a methodology for estimating a portion of the economic benefits of the NPS's educational programs. A full estimate would include estimates of the NPS's leveraging role as an organizer and facilitator of the educational efforts of its partners. It would also include a measure of the long-term impact of place-based education on the educational achievements of students. While both of these are significant, they are also very difficult to quantify. Thus we focus on the direct use value of NPS educational services to users, acknowledging that our final estimate is a highly conservative measure of the likely economic values. More fundamentally, it is important to recognize that a necessary condition for all these services to be produced is the sustained stewardship of the underlying natural and cultural resources. For example, place-based learning about the battle of Gettysburg is not possible without preservation and curation of the battlefield itself. Therefore, in its broadest sense, the entire NPS system constitutes an educational resource to the nation.

Our approach starts with a detailed case study of the Golden Gate National Recreation Area (GGNRA), an NPS area over 200,000 acres in size on the west side of San Francisco Bay in California. To provide an order of magnitude estimate of the educational value provided by the entire NPS and its partners, we then generalize these results to all units of the NPS, while acknowledging the limitations of such an approach.

This approach yields a conservative estimate of annual value for NPS educational services of between $949 million to $1.22 billion. This contrasts with annual expenditures of some $45 million (Washburn, 2016) by the NPS on educational activities. The economic value thus implies a 21–27 times annual return on investment. In reality, the long-term return on investment is likely substantially higher, as learning often provides the student and society with a lifetime of benefits.

Methodology

In this chapter we expand upon the human capital development element in Figure 1.1 (Choi and Marlowe valuation framework) presented in Chapter 1. This expansion is illustrated in Figure 5.1.

We have identified two main avenues through which NPS facilitates learning: (a) 'on-site programming' and (b) 'educational materials and resources', as shown in Figure 5.1.

(a) on-site programming is defined as educational programs that NPS and its partners design and provide for visitors to the parks and historic sites. Such programs range from 'light-touch' single interactions with interpretive staff to sustained yearlong youth leadership development

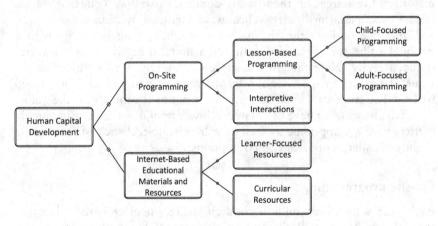

Figure 5.1 Human capital development framework

initiatives. On-site programming includes lesson-based programming, in which a curriculum or unit plan with specific objectives is used, and interpretive interactions, which are spontaneous interactions between rangers and the public

Examples of on-site programs include:

- K-12 student field trips within parks
- Youth leadership development programs
- Interpretive talks and tours by rangers
- Teacher professional development within and focused on the parks

(b) NPS also produces educational materials and resources for use by the public at large, including those not visiting park units. Examples include:

- K-12 curricula linking historical and natural themes present in the parks to the Common Core
- Virtual tours of National Parks
- Virtual experiences such as watching wildlife on a webcam
- Virtual exhibits, videos, and games explaining historical, natural, and cultural concepts
- Other materials designed for classroom use by teachers

In this chapter, we focus on web or internet-based educational resources when exploring educational materials and resources developed by NPS. We do this because internet-based materials represent a large fraction of the NPS resources accessible to non-visitors. These include learner-focused resources, for consumption by the end-user, and curricular resources, designed for use by teachers. Learner-focused resources are defined here as those NPS resources intended for use by all internet users. They include the majority of resources on the nps.gov domain, as well as YouTube videos, iTunes U courses, third-party webcams, and national webinars.

Figure 5.2 outlines the approach we've taken to aggregating up to a national value for education in the NPS units, using the two categories outlined above. Note that for on-site programming, we've multiplied the value of services in the GGNRA by the ratio of national students served to GGNRA students served to arrive at a national estimate of the value. For each element, we have calculated a 'lower bound' estimate using highly conservative assumptions, as well as a 'moderate-realistic' estimate using slightly broader, more realistic assumptions.

On-site programming

Each year some seven million children engage in place-based education through the National Parks and its partners. Millions more adults also

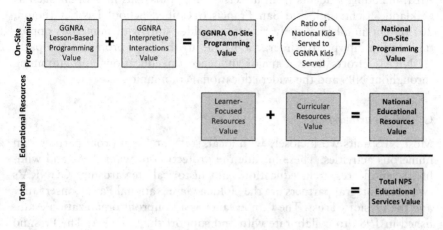

Figure 5.2 Valuation methodology for NPS-provided education

engage in place-based educational programming and interactions through the parks.

The GGNRA: a case study of on-site programming

The GGNRA comprises several unique sites that total more than 200,000 acres on the west side of the San Francisco Bay. These include the Muir Woods, Alcatraz Island, the Marin headlands, the Presidio, Ocean Beach, Fort Funston, Tomales Bay, and other well-known locations (NPS, 2016). With over 15 million annual recreational visitors, the GGNRA is the most visited NPS unit, accounting for over 5% of NPS visitors nationwide (NPS, 2016). The GGNRA covers a wide variety of natural landscapes, including redwood forests, beaches, and coastal chaparral, as well as cultural and historical sites.

We selected GGNRA for this case study due to the innovative educational programs that GGNRA and its partners provide. Most youth programs are aligned with the Common Core and local curricula, ensuring that their services are complementary to the classroom experience. GGNRA's professional development for educators is recognized as a leading national program (Fonfa, 2015).

In addition, GGNRA considers itself a 'partnership park', working with multiple non-profit and government partners to provide a vast suite of educational services. In this way, the park is able to augment its capacity to pursue its own mission, often in a way that is 'a little different to what we would ordinarily think of on our own' (Levitt, 2013).

Finally, the proximity to a metropolitan area and the volume of visitors make the GGNRA an ideal case study. The youth educational programs serve hundreds of thousands of students from across the San Francisco Bay

Area, including students from underserved populations in districts such as Oakland, Richmond, and San Francisco Unified School District (Fonfa, 2015). The number of daily visitors provides staff with numerous opportunities for interpretive interaction. Due to the high profile of the park, GGNRA's efforts have a major influence on educational programming throughout NPS and the wider educational community.

GGNRA partnerships

Most NPS units work closely with local, state, and non-profit partners[1] on numerous activities. These include the protection of watersheds and wildlife, scientific research, education, and historical stewardship. GGNRA's two most integral partners are the Golden Gate National Park Conservancy and the Presidio Trust. The Conservancy is a nonprofit organization established in 1981 to collaborate with and support the GGNRA. The Presidio Trust was created in 1996 to 'preserve the areas of the Presidio, a former military barracks at the northern tip of the San Francisco Peninsula' (The Presidio Trust, 2015).

Many other organizations also operate in partnership with GGNRA including the San Francisco Unified School District (SFUSD), which partners closely with GGNRA and runs a science center in Fort Funston.

On-site programming at GGNRA

In partnership with organizations such as the Conservancy and the Presidio Trust, NPS provides a wide range of on-site programming[2]. As illustrated in Figure 5.3 a spectrum of on-site programming that represents different levels of engagement by NPS and the participants. These range from 'single-touch' interpretive interactions to a yearlong youth leadership course. The position of an educational activity along this 'intensity spectrum' can be important in assessing its economic value. Less intensive programs may

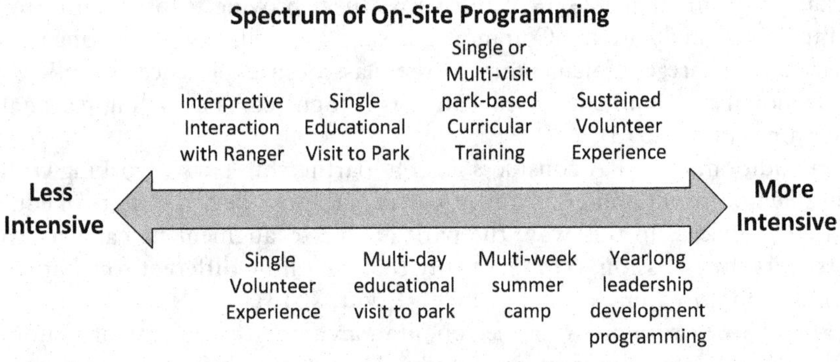

Figure 5.3 Spectrum of on-site programming intensity

provide specific academic benefit to young people and perhaps lead to better environmental/cultural stewardship and greater enjoyment of park facilities. Longer, sustained engagement programming provides broader academic and stewardship benefits, and also includes a developmental or leadership value that itself provides the individual with benefits throughout their schooling and career. We think this spectrum is a useful way to conceptualize on-site programming and tie it to economic valuation. However, the data requirements, especially for the longer, sustained engagement and programming requires repeated longitudinal surveys of participants to measure the full participant benefits. Such data is not available for GGNRA, and therefore our valuations presented below are limited by the available data.

NPS-led programs

The key lesson-based youth program run by the NPS at GGNRA is 'Parks as Classrooms', a set of 14 inquiry-based programs that include both classroom and on-site lessons, and are linked to the California common core. The programs serve children from kindergarten to 12th grade, and span subjects such as ecology, history, and geology.

Each program includes off-site learning that takes place prior to and subsequent to the park visit. GGNRA trains the teacher to present a pre-lesson or sends a representative into the classroom. In 2014–2015 a total of 7,677 students throughout the Bay Area received roughly 18,906 student hours of this type of programming (GGNRA, 2015a, 2015b)[3]. NPS at GGNRA also provides educational programming to adults. These programs are designed to help teachers improve their instructional skills using Park themes and resources.

Finally, a significant part of the educational experience provided by NPS takes place through what we term interpretive interactions. Examples include informal learning (such as spontaneous discussions and questions to rangers and trained park volunteers), formal interpretation (organized ranger programs and interpretative tours), and junior ranger programs, internships and volunteer opportunities (Koenen, 2015). There were 255,000 informal interpretive interactions and 95,000 formal interpretive interactions in GGNRA during the 2014–2015 fiscal year (GGNRA, 2015)[4], which we estimate provided 158,000 person-hours of education.

Volunteer and internship opportunities provide more sustained opportunities for interpretive interactions at the GGNRA. In total, GGNRA hosted 137 interns in the fiscal year 2014–2015, for a total of almost 110,000 hours. Many of these opportunities are designed specifically for volunteers' professional and personal development, and are highly sought-after (Fonfa, 2015). During the 2014–2015 year, 27,000 volunteers recorded over 494,000 hours of volunteer time. (GGNRA, 2015)

In sum, we estimate that a total of 377,349 attendees engaged in 763,558 hours of interpretive interactions within the park.

Partner programs with GGNRA

The Conservancy and Presidio Trust partner with NPS to lead a number of major youth programs in the GGNRA. These youth programs provide opportunities for long periods of engagements, programs to develop youth leaders who are invested in their local environment (Pon, 2015); a year-long leadership program in which students meet twice per week to learn about parks and environmental issues, and other programs which include summer camps and internships. During the fiscal year 2012–2013 (the most recent year for which data is available), youth-level lesson-based programming reached 20,000 students and was responsible for an estimated 113,000 student hours of education (Barzanji, 2013).

The Conservancy and Presidio Trust also offer adult-level and general-level lesson-based programs. These include professional development for educators and community leadership training. In the 2012–2013 fiscal year, this adult- and general-level education reached at least 4,000 people for an estimated total of at least 17,000 person hours (Barzanji, 2013). Finally, interpretive interactions run through the Conservancy and Presidio Trust include interactions with the public at the Presidio nursery, as well as various educational fairs and festivals. In 2012–2013, some 4,000 people spent approximately 19,000 person-hours in Conservancy and Presidio Trust-supported interpretive interaction (Barzanji, 2013).

Numerous other partners work with GGNRA to provide educational programming. Such programs are primarily in the category of lesson-based youth programming. An example includes the SFUSD Environmental Science Center based at Fort Funston: environmental science day and overnight programming for 3,614 students across the district in the 2014–2015 school year. Adult volunteer programs include 14,508 hours (Wojcik, 2015).

Summary of programming at GGNRA

The educational programming provided by the NPS, the Conservancy, the Presidio Trust, and other partners is summarized in Table 5.1. In total, we estimate over 453,000 participants engaged in more than 1.1 million hours of free educational programming and interactions within and through the GGNRA.

Estimating the value of GGNRA's on-site programming

We estimate the value for a year's worth of educational programs provided by GGNRA and its partners by using mixed methods of replacement cost estimation and use value benefits transfer. We applied a cost-based methodology for youth and adult lesson-based programming, using the cost of similar education in the public realm. This indicates how much local or national education providers would have to pay to replace the educational

Table 5.1 On-site programming at the GGNRA

	Lesson-based child		Lesson-based adult		Interpretive		Total	
	Participants	Person hours	Participants	Person hours	Participants	Person hours	Participants	Person hours
NPS	7,677	18,906	1,149	3,130	377,349	763,558	386,175	785,594
Conservancy/ Presidio Trust	20,265	113,997	4,275	17,173	4,018	18,842	28,558	150,011
Other partners (w/out fees)	21,536	123,404	—	—	17,437	48,808	38,973	172,212
Total (w/out fees)	49,478	256,307	5,424	20,303	398,804	831,207	453,706	1,107,817

services provided by GGNRA and NPS if the NPS did not provide these educational opportunities, thus providing a basis for their value. Since the majority of participants attending youth and adult lesson-based programming attended through their school systems in replacement of or in augmentation to their existing educational programming, we feel confident that this GGNRA programming would have required replacement in some manner and at a similar cost.

Use value is the direct value to a subject from the use of a good or service. For interpretive interactions, we have transferred the estimated use value of experiences that are similar to those interactions, such as guided walks and curated visits to aquariums and arboretums[5].

This valuation methodology is very conservative. First, we have included only the replacement cost and use value of this programming, omitting the special and unique features of place-based education at the GGNRA. Second, we have not differentiated between the value of 'single-touch' and longer-term programming—even though we believe those who participate in longer park programs derive much higher value. Additionally, we have not attempted to estimate the possibly life-changing benefits that may accrue to a number of participants (such as a higher likelihood to graduate from high school, or improved lifelong fitness). This kind of study would likely produce a much higher estimate of value[6].

Lesson-based youth programming

Lesson-based youth programming often replaces or augments K-12 schooling. For this reason, it is possible to estimate a range of value by calculating the cost that school districts would have to pay to replace this lost education if the programming did not exist. As the parklands are located within and surrounding SFUSD and many of the programs serve youth attending schools in the district, we have used the SFUSD budget to estimate the cost per hour of education. Based on the SFUSD general fund budget for 2015–2016 (SFUSD, 2016), we estimate the direct replacement cost of 256,000 person-hours of youth lesson-based programming at $2.7 million, our lowest-bound estimate. Our upper-bound estimate is $4.6 million and is based on including additional SFUSD school funding in the form of financial assistance to schools with high numbers of low-income families (e.g., Title 1 funds) when calculating the replacement cost of an hour of youth-based programming.

Lesson-based adult programming

Much of the lesson-based adult programming takes the form of professional development (PD) for educators, which is a service provided in all school districts. We estimated this value in two ways. First, we used the average of costs to private companies and to districts to provide an hour of PD, in 2015 real dollars. This equaled approximately $45 per teacher hour. Multiplied by the 20,303 person-hours of adult lesson-based programming provided by GGNRA, we calculate a lower bound replacement cost value of roughly $900,000. Taking into account PD planning and implementation costs, we estimate the replacement value as $1.3 million. This figure is based on the hourly cost of Philadelphia public schools, which trained 3,500 people for 220,000 person-hours' worth of PD at an hourly development and implementation cost of $64.21.

Interpretive interactions

'Interpretive' education is frequently in the form of interaction with existing Park programming, such as guided experiences and interpretative information provided by Park rangers. Accordingly, we have estimated the value of these experiences by using the Recreational Use Value (Rosenberger, 2015) database to transfer benefits for similar activities. These activities included visiting nature centers, arboretums, aquariums, cultural sites, and historic sites. Using this database and those activities, we calculate an average benefit of $7.86 per person-hour of interpretive interaction, indicating a value of $6.5 million for these interactions at GGNRA. However, the vast majority of visitors to National Parks do not interact with rangers, but still use and benefit from interpretive exhibits. In our case study of GGNRA, of the 15 million people who visited the GGNRA in 2015 (NPS, 2016), only 345,000 (2%) had interactions with rangers. We have assumed that a further 3.75 million–5 million people (25–33% of visitors) benefited from interpretive exhibits but interacted with those exhibits for just five minutes, which is far less time than they would have devoted if they had spoken to a ranger. Based on these assumptions, we estimate that the value of interpretive interactions is between $9.0 million and $9.4 million[7].

As displayed in Table 5.2 our conservative estimate for on-site programming at GGNRA is valued at $12.6 million–$15.4 million per year. This estimate excludes programming provided on a fee basis.

Table 5.2 Value estimates of on-site programs at the GGNRA[1]

Programming type	Lowest-bound estimate (million)	Moderate-realistic estimate (million)
Youth lesson-based programming	$ 2.7	$ 4.7
Adult lesson-based programming	$ 0.9	$ 1.3
Interpretive interactions	$ 9.0	$ 9.4
Total	$ 12.6	$ 15.4

[1] Note that numbers in table may not add exactly up due to rounding.

Estimating nationwide value of on-site programming

Nationwide, seven million schoolchildren are served by National Parks-based educational programs from the NPS and partners (Chen, 2016). This is about 71 times the number of students that the GGNRA and partners serve. Consequently, we can estimate the value of educational programming nationwide by multiplying our estimated value of GGNRA programming by 71. This would place the value for on-site programming alone to a range of $895 million–$1.1 billion[8]. This valuation estimation process is displayed in Figure 5.4.

One possible concern with using GGNRA as a baseline is that it is considered a leader within the National Parks System. However, while GGNRA is a leader it is not unique among NPS units. Numerous NPS units have extensive educational programs, including Cuyahoga Valley NP, Santa Monica NRA, Lowell National Historical Park, Rock Creek Park in Washington DC, Great Smokey Mountains NP, Independence National Historical Park in Philadelphia and dozens of others. Similar to GGNRA, these NPS units have adopted a partnership model and offer extensive programming, including youth education, teacher training, summer programs, interpretation, and a wide range of activities customized to their local environments. Therefore, we feel it is reasonable to apply the simple methodology that preceded for valuing on-site programming.

Internet-based educational materials and resources

NPS also provides educational benefits to those who cannot visit NPS units in person. These benefits include web-based programs, educational resources and websites, webcams, films, teacher lesson materials, and other services. This section estimates the value provided by NPS educational resources when delivered using these modes.

We focused primarily on the provision of internet-based educational materials and services. NPS internet-based user-focused interpretive resources were used for between 209 million and 368 million person-minutes. We also find that curricular resources were used to create from 740,000 to 2.5 million lessons. Thus, we estimate the value of a year's worth of use of these educational resources to be between $54 million and $124 million. This section examines the NPS's provision of each of these types of resources and outlines our methodology for estimating their value.

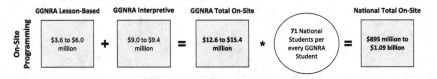

Figure 5.4 Calculation for total value of on-site educational programming

Learner-focused interpretive resources

Learner-focused interpretive resources are defined here as NPS resources intended for use by all internet users. These include the majority of resources on the nps.gov domain, as well as YouTube videos, iTunes U courses, third-party webcams, and national webinars.

NPS.gov

When entering the nps.gov domain a user can choose to search for an individual park, or select from a menu of systemwide options (including 'Discover History', 'Explore Nature', 'Get Involved', 'Working with Communities', 'Teachers', 'Kids', and 'About Us').

NPS.gov provides multiple cross-park/national resources to educate users, compiled by the NPS including 'Historical and Cultural Programs', 'People, Places, and Stories', 'Nature', 'Teachers', and 'Kids' (see NPS, 2016a–f in references for specifics). Each NPS unit homepage also contains educational resources for learning about the particular NPS unit, including 'News', 'Photos and Multimedia', 'History and Culture', 'Nature', and 'Kids and Youth' (e.g., https://www.nps.gov/yell/learn/index.htm; also see NPS, 2016a–f for specifics). There are subsites dedicated specifically to historical and cultural programs, heritage areas, historic preservation tax incentives, biographies, wildlife and other materials that help 'tell the American Story'. A dedicated section of the domain provides access to NPS-based curricula for teachers.

Using Yellowstone National Park as an example, we found a range of park-specific educational resources, including multimedia, a YouTube channel, audio postcards (with links to sounds of the park), and eight different virtual tours (we purposely omit basic touristic information such as maps, planning a visit, and operation hours, which we do not classify as educational).

YouTube

External to the nps.gov domain, NPS and its various operating branches maintain at least 118 YouTube channels[9]. These channels cover a wide range of NPS units, including National Parks, National Monuments, National Historical Parks and National Battlefields, and National Wild and Scenic Rivers. They also include channels for NPS-wide programs.

Podcasts

Podcasts and video 'courses' on iTunes and iTunes U provide another education channel. The NPS has created at least 29 non-iTunes U podcast channels, with 442 video and audio podcast episodes. A further 88 NPS iTunes U channels provide roughly 950 videos organized around specific themes[10].

Other original content

A major avenue for online education is through webinars and online training. These include instructional courses in historical preservation, landmark protection, preservation of battlefields, and a wide variety of other
topics. The NPS Cultural Resources, Partnerships and Science Directorate
is a leader in producing these events. While we do not have participation
numbers for the majority of these, there is evidence that some are widely
attended.

Quantifying use of learner-focused interpretive resources

To value the use of these internet resources over a single fiscal year, we
first aggregate the amount of user educational time spent with them. This
was based on identifying the number of sessions spent by individuals using
the resource and the average minutes spent per session. The total number
of minutes was estimated by multiplying the number of sessions times the
average minutes. The methodology and assumptions we used to derive a
monetary value for these activities are outlined in the following section.

NPS.gov

In the fiscal year 2014–2015, the nps.gov domain as a whole was accessed
for 137.8 million sessions averaging 3.5 minutes in duration. We have further filtered this number to the subset of site users who visited an educational URL during their site visit using search terms described in this
endnote[11]. This filtering mechanism returned 37.9 million educational sessions averaging 9.6 minutes, a total of 345 million minutes of user engagement. Educational users spent almost three times as long on the site as the
average NPS.gov user, indicating that they engaged more deeply with the
content. We have used this number of minutes as our moderate realistic
bound.

Our lower-bound estimate includes users who visited the educational
subdomains along with visits to the trip-planning parts of the website
(including 'Find a Park' and 'Plan your Visit'). Those who visited educational subdomains spent 57% of their session time on them, meaning that
43% was spent on other parts of the site. To address this, we subtracted the
amount of time spent on non-educational pages by those users (see search
terms used to identify non-educational pages in this endnote[12]). The resulting estimate is 196 million minutes overall.

YouTube

The 3,686 NPS videos found on YouTube have received a combined 22.3
million views over the course of their beginning to the time of the background

research for this chapter (11/20/2015). Due to the lack of specific longitudinal data on views over time, we assume an even number of views per year over the course of a video's life[13]. To be conservative we eliminated all views of 30 seconds or less to eliminate inadvertent or superficial viewing. This is cut off is consistent with Beck's (2015) research on a similar topic. Our resulting estimate is that these YouTube videos were viewed approximately 3.9 million times over the course of the fiscal year 2014–2015. The volume of videos posted by multiple parks made it difficult to calculate an average video length. A quick survey of the highly used channels of two California NPs found varying lengths for videos[14]. The GGNRA channel posted public service announcements as short as 10 seconds long, with an average length of all 65 videos on the channel of 2 minutes and 38 seconds. We used this average number as our lower-bound estimate for video length, equal to 12.4 million minutes watched.

By contrast, the Yosemite NP channel, which is the most-viewed channel in the National Park System, posted longer science-oriented videos with an average length of 6.24 minutes. To calculate a realistic estimate, therefore, we assumed that the best number was the average between the GGNRA and Yosemite video lengths, for an estimate of 4 minutes and 31 seconds, which is close to the overall average of YouTube views (Sysomous, 2010). Using this estimate, the annual user time for NPS YouTube videos is 21.2 million minutes watched.

Podcasts

Given known download numbers of other signpost podcasts, we estimate that the NPS podcasts have been downloaded 1.65 million times, or ~300,000 times per year over five years[15]. Given an average podcast length of around five minutes, we estimate that between 1 million (conservative) and 1.5 million (moderate) minutes' worth of content were consumed by NPS podcast users during 2015.

Valuation of learner-focused interpretive resources

To determine a value for the use of internet-based education from NPS, we attempted to value the benefits from time spent on these educational resources. While this type of valuation does not account for the longer-term educational benefits derived from using these resources, it provides a baseline of possible value.

Economists Goolsbee and Klenow (2006) suggested a methodology for calculating the benefits realized by users viewing an internet site by accounting for the opportunity cost of the time spent using it. They report that in the year of their data (2006), the average internet subscriber spent 7.7 hours per week, or 400 hours per year, of leisure time on the internet[16]. In that same year, that 400 hours per year of use created a benefit for each

Table 5.3 Learner-focused interpretive resource values

Value of learner-focused interpretative resource use			
Resource	Minutes spent on internet-based NPS education (lower-bound estimate)	Minutes spent on internet-based NPS education (moderate-realistic estimate)	Economic value using consumer surplus methodology ($ millions)
nps.gov	96.0	345.0	$33–$58
YouTube	12.4	21.3	$2.1–$3.6
Podcasts	1.0	1.5	$0.2–$0.3
Total	208.8	367.7	$35.3–$61.9

user ranging from 1.9–2.9% of full income, depending on a user's income and the assumed income elasticity of demand (Goolsbee & Klenow, 2006). For our lower-bound estimate, we used the 1.9% of income. Since 90% of nps.gov sessions had U.S. internet protocol (IP) addresses we apply the 1.9% to current U.S. per capita GDP data as a proxy for income. Performing these calculations we estimated range of $35.2 million–$61.9 million in Table 5.3 for the value provided by NPS internet resources for the 2014–2015 fiscal year.

Curricular resources

NPS designs special curricular resources for teachers via the nps.gov domain. Because this activity is a distinct educational undertaking of the NPS, we have completed a separate valuation for this portion of the website.

The Teachers section of the website is home to 499 lesson plans that cover a wide array of themes including biodiversity, economic history, and cultural customs of native peoples (NPS, 2015). There are also lesson plans that exist outside the teacher portal, on the 'For Teachers' section of individual Parks' web pages.

An estimated 2.3 million users accessed curricular sections of the website in Fiscal Year 2014-2015 through 2.5 million sessions. This represents 16% of all time these users spent on the site during these sessions. According to Google analytics, around 740,000 PDF documents have been downloaded (and therefore likely used) from curricular sections of the site during that period. To value this service, we used the download figure (740,000) as a lower bound estimate for lesson plan use. We adopted the number of web sessions (2.5 million) as our moderate estimate.

Developing classroom curriculum is complex and time-consuming. A reasonable approach to value this effort is to estimate the time it takes for a teacher to create a lesson plan and then to estimate the value of the saved time. Teachers in two separate online forums estimated that for each hour's worth of new lessons that they teach, they spend between 30 minutes and two hours in lesson planning[17]. We have conservatively used one hour as the estimate of the time necessary for lesson planning. We consider this the time saved by a teacher, subtracting from it the seven minutes (.13 hours) on average that users were on the website (so as not to double count that time as part of lesson preparation) to come to a final calculation of .87 hours saved per lesson used.

When estimating the value of teacher time saved, we convert the average salary to a wage rate as a proxy for the value of that time to a teacher (see this endnote for a discussion of the strengths and weaknesses of this approach for teachers[18]). The national average salary of elementary school teachers is $56,860 (US News, 2016).To convert this salary to an hourly wage rate to value time, we need to divide this average salary by hours worked. Of course, most teachers do not work in the classroom a full year as they typically have a 10-week summer vacation. They do work an average of 53 hours per week during the school year itself (Washington Post, 2012). Using 53 hours a week times 38 weeks provides slightly more than a 2,000-hour work year. Using 2,000 hours a year, we estimate in Table 5.4 that the value of the time saved for teachers through NPS providing these resources is between $18.3 million and $61.8 million.

Neither of these valuation methods fully represents the value of the unique materials contained on the NPS teacher portal. Based on the average class size (30) in the Scholastic survey (2016), we estimate that between 22 million and 33 million students nationwide were able to benefit from these materials each year.

Summary of internet-based educational materials and resources

Overall, we find that the online educational materials and experiences provided by the NPS provide a range of possible value, from a conservative estimate of $54 million to a more moderate estimate of $124 million. While these figures are small relative to those for on-site programming, they still demonstrate that online learning and resources are an extremely valuable piece of the NPS educational portfolio (Figure 5.5).

Table 5.4 Lesson plan value—conservative and moderate realistic estimate

	Lessons used	Time saved planning per lesson (hours)	Teacher salary/ hour	Total value
Conservative estimate	740,000	0.87	$28.43	$18.3 million
Moderate estimate	2.5 million	0.87	$28.43	$61.8 million

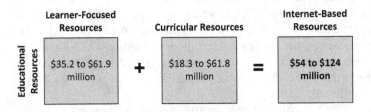

Figure 5.5 Valuing internet-based educational resources

Conclusion

The economic value of the educational programming, resources, and services provided by the National Parks to students, teachers, and internet users is substantial. Data and other limitations make it difficult to calculate a comprehensive estimate of this value. However, our methodology shown in Figure 5.6 indicates that that the direct use value alone of these educational services and resources lies in a range of $949 million–$1.22 billion, with the lower bound based on extremely conservative assumptions.

Our valuation contrasts with the NPS's annual Education and Interpretation budget of just $45 million (Washburn, 2016) across the NPS on educational activities. A comparison of our estimate of the annual economic value to the NPS Education and Interpretation budget implies a 21–27 times annual return on investment.

Two steps can be taken to further refine our valuation:

1   Fund and conduct experimental research on the effects of educational programming and resources at multiple NPS units to better understand

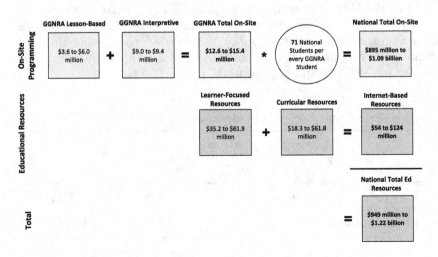

Figure 5.6 Total roadmap of educational value produced by NPS

the educational and social benefits of NPS Education and Interpretation. For example, comparing graduation rates of students who have participated in NPS on-site programming to those that have not.

2 Better catalog the educational programming occurring at individual NPS units throughout the country.

We hope the methods outlined in this chapter will encourage others to estimate the educational values of their individual NPS units. One day NPS will better be able to have a more precise estimate of the economic value of the many facets of NPS educational resources.

While valuation is not an end in and of itself, it can aid in decision-making regarding budgets. Analysis can also identify positive external benefits produced by public sector actions that improve the lives of large numbers of citizens. Education is certainly an example of this, one that pays long-term dividends that we have been unable to quantify in this chapter.

As we begin the second century of the NPS, we hope this chapter, and the methods contained herein, will lead to more studies to demonstrate the wide range of economic benefits created by the NPS's extraordinary education programs and resources.

Notes

1 NPS is distinctive among federal agencies in the scale of these partnerships, which enable NPS to leverage its assets to provide 'cooperative programming' (Choi-Marlowe, 2012).

2 We have noted some programs led by partners who charge fees for their services, but these are excluded from our calculations of value because of the complexity of assigning an economic value to end-users.

3 This does not count the number of hours dedicated to these units prior to those students interacting with park rangers, which is likely much higher.

4 There were also a large number of public interactions through visitor centers that were logged. However, we judged it likely that many of these interactions involved non-educational purposes and thus excluded them from the data-set.

5 We note that our use value estimates utilize benefits transfer methodology without the knowledge that conditions in the valuation site and the transfer site are the same. We have attempted to address this by taking the average of use values across multiple studies of interpretive interactions with nature.

6 For example, the average wage per week for high-school graduates $678 and unemployment is 5.4% vs. a weekly wage of $493 for non-high school graduate and unemployment is 8% (US Bureau of Labor Statistics, 2016).

7 Note that we have excluded the value of fee-based programming, even though most of the sponsors subsidize or offer scholarships to low-income students. If we were to assume that just 20% of fee-based hours were performed on this basis, it would add an additional $1 million to the value.

8 Note that these totals are lower than the $14.2 billion value for NPS's education programs developed using stated preference choice experiment methodology to determine the total economic value (TEV) of the NPS in Chapter 2 of this book. This difference arises because TEV includes both direct use value and non-use/passive use - in other words, the value that non-participants derive from simply knowing that such education programs exist. The current paper measures the direct use value to the students, parents, teachers and other users which can

be estimated at some $894 million–$1.1 billion. By contrast, the TEV study in Chapter 2 estimated what the American public would pay for the NPS and its partners to provide educational experiences and programming to 4.1 million schoolchildren. Based on the demographics of respondents, only a fraction of the survey respondents likely had school age children. Thus, most of the TEV of $14.2 billion for education was non-use or passive-use value—values that people receive from knowing that NPS educational programming on natural, cultural, and historic aspects of America are provided. With regard to educating children there is a degree of paternalistic altruism in that it is the amount a person will pay for education for others children because they personally want those children to have this particular educational experience. Existence and altruism are the same element that often results in a majority of citizens voting for school bonds, despite the fact that a majority of voters do not have nor expect to have school-age children.

9 This number represents the number of official NPS channels that could be found on YouTube on 11/20/2015 using the search terms 'National Park', 'NPS', 'National Park Service', 'National Monument', 'National Historical Park', 'National Battlefield', 'Scenic River'.

10 These numbers represent the number of official NPS podcasts and video casts that could be found on iTunes in a search for the following terminology on 11/27/2015: 'National Park', 'NPS', 'National Park Service', 'National Monument', 'National Historical Park', 'National Battlefield', 'Scenic River'.

11 This set of terms included in the url search in Google Analytics is as follows: '/kids/', '/history', 'nature.', '/webcams', '/learn/', 'focus.', 'photosmultimedia', '/news/', '/learnandexplore/','/aboutus/'. These terms were chosen because they were associated with the root urls from the 'Learn and Explore' section of the nps.gov domain, as opposed to the 'Plan Your Visit' section.

12 We estimated the non-educational time spent on the site by users who accessed educational resources by searching a list of the top 1000 urls visited by those users for terms that appear mostly in the non-education-based sections of the domain. These include 'Find a Park' and 'Index', the latter of which appears in the urls of individual park homepages. We then calculated the proportion of time spent at those non-educational urls by visitors to educational subdomains (43%) and removed it from the sample.

13 There is ample research on video popularity trends to indicate that this even distribution of views over time is likely not an accurate assumption (Chowdury, 2010), but given the lack of longitudinal data on the videos in question, the assumption must suffice for the given calculations.

14 This sample of videos was taken from the following YouTube sites on 11/20/2015: www.youtube.com/user/GoldenGateNPS and www.youtube.com/user/yosemitenationalpark.

15 This American Life, which averages around 1 million downloads per episode over the course of 573 episodes (http://www.thisamericanlife.org/podcast) has 19,421 reviews, for an average of about 30,000 downloads per review. Applying the lower bound ratio of 20,000 downloads per review to the 55 reviews across NPS podcasts, we come to a figure of 1,100,000 downloads across podcasts. On average the podcasts have been available for 5 years, so, given a linear download trend (which we know may not be the case), we can assume ~220,000 podcast downloads per year. Using 30,000 as an upper bound, we estimate that the NPS podcasts have been downloaded 1.65 million times, or roughly 330,000 times per year over 5 years.

16 We recognize that there has been a substantial increase in internet usage since 2006. Part of this is no doubt due to the introduction of smart phones in 2007, which allowed mobile access to the internet. How much of mobile use is a net

addition versus displacement of desktop/laptop internet use is not known. But we would suspect that smart phones have resulted in a significant increase in internet usage.

17 The forums are http://forums.atozteacherstuff.com/index.php?threads/how-long-does-it-typically-take-you-to-lesson-plan.120254/ and https://www.reddit.com/r/Teachers/comments/3h6b3a/how_long_does_it_take_you_to_lesson_plan/.

18 Note that most teachers are not compensated by the hour, and thus may not equate the value of their time at their average hourly fully loaded cost—especially as many teachers are known for working long hours. It may also be that teachers would replace one set of work with another set of work, in effect simply increasing the amount of work they get done instead of providing them with more leisure time. Regardless, the time-valuation methodology provides a valuable estimate of the possible worth of NPS lesson plans to teachers. However, if that time comes out of what would have otherwise been leisure time, there is some evidence from time budget studies that individuals value another hour of leisure time as greater than the wage rate. Nonetheless the wage rate is often used by economists to value time in a wide variety of settings (e.g., transportation time savings).

References

Barzanji, T. 2013. Combined Data on GGNPC Program Use [Data-set]. San Francisco, CA.

Beck, M. 2015. What's a video view? On Facebook, only 3 seconds vs. 30 at YouTube. *Marketing Land*. Retrieved 12 May 2015 from http://marketingland.com/whats-a-video-view-on-facebook-only-3-seconds-vs-30-at-youtube-128311.

Chen, M. 2016. Learning in the 21st Century: Education in America and the National Park Service.

Choi, F. and T. Marlowe. 2012. *The Value of America's Greatest Idea*. Cambridge, MA: Policy Analysis Exercise for the Harvard Kennedy School.

Chowdury, G. 2010. From digital libraries to digital preservation research: the importance of users and context. *Journal of Documentation*66 (2): 207–223.

Fonfa, L. 2015. Education Specialist, GGNRA. (T. Marlowe, Interviewer, 18 August 2015.)

Golden Gate National Recreation Area (GGNRA). 2015a. GGNRA Parks as Classrooms Student Attendance [Dataset]. San Francisco, CA.

Golden Gate National Recreation Area (GGNRA). 2015b. SIR 12 Months GOGA Roll-up [Data-set]. San Francisco, CA.

Goolsbee, A. and P. J. Klenow. 2006. *Valuing Consumer Products by the Time Spent Using Them: An Application to the Internet*. Cambridge, MA: National Bureau of Economic Research.

Koenen, M. 2015. Supervisor of Interpretative Facilities and Operations. (T. Marlowe, Interviewer, 15 September 2015.)

Levitt, H. 2013. Chief of Communications and Partnerships. (T. Barzanji, Interviewer, 31 July 2013.)

Lieberman, G. A. and L. L. Hoody. 1998. *Closing the Achievement Gap: Using the Environment as an Integrating Context for Learning*. Poway, CA: State Education and Environment Round Table; Science Wizards.

NPS. 2015. Teacher Resources. Retrieved 20 November 2015 from NPS.gov: https://www.nps.gov/teachers/teacher-resources.htm.

NPS. 2016a. About Us. Retrieved from NPS.gov: http://www.nps.gov/aboutus/index.htm.

NPS. 2016b. Golden Gate National Recreation Area. Retrieved 23 May 2016 from NPS.gov: http://www.nps.gov/goga.

NPS. 2016c. Integrated Resource Management Applications Portal. Retrieved 23 May 2016 from NPS.gov: https://irma.nps.gov/Portal.

NPS. 2016d. National Park Service. Retrieved 10 October 2016 from http://www.nps.gov.

NPS. 2016e. National Park Service Visitor Use Statistics. Retrieved 19 November 2016 from Integrated Resource Management Applications: https://irma.nps.gov/Stats/.

NPS. 2016f. Yellowstone: Learn about the Park. Retrieved 1 November 2016 from NPS.gov: https://www.nps.gov/yell/learn/index.htm

Pon, D. 2015. Youth Development Coordinator, Golden Gate National Parks Conservancy. (T. Marlowe, Interviewer, 29 June 2015.)

Rosenberger, R. 2015. Recreational Use Values Database [Data-set]. Retrieved November 2015 from Oregon State University College of Forestry: http://recvaluation.forestry.oregonstate.edu/.

SFUSD. 2016. SFUSD 15–16 Budget. Retrieved from SFUSD San Francisco Public Schools: http://www.sfusd.edu/en/about-sfusd/budget.html.

Scholastic. 2016. Every Kid in a Park. Retrieved from Scholastic: www.scholastic.com/everykid.

Sysomos. 2010. Inside YouTube Video Statistics. Retrieved from Sysomos: https://sysomos.com/reports/youtube-video-statistics.

The Presidio Trust. 2015. Mission and History. Retrieved 20 September 2015 from Presidio.gov: www.presidio.gov/about/Pages/mission-history.

U.S. Bureau of Labor Statistics. 2016. Earnings and Unemployment Rates by Educational Attainment. Retrieved 15 March 2016 from BLS Employment Projections: http://data.bls.gov/cgi-bin/print.pl/emp/ep_table_001.htm.

U.S. News. 2016. High School Teacher Salary. Retrieved from Best Jobs U.S. News Ranking: http://money.usnews.com/careers/best-jobs/high-school-teacher/salary.

Washburn, J. 2013. Director for Interpretation, Education, and Volunteers. (T. Barzanji, Interviewer, December 19 2013.)

Washington Post. 2012. Survey: Teachers Work 53 Hours Per Week on Average. Retrieved 16 March 2012 from https://www.washingtonpost.com/blogs/answer-sheet/post/survey-teachers-work-53-hours-per-week-on-average/2012/03/16/gIQAqGxYGS_blog.html.

Wojcik, L. 2015. Director, SFUSD Environmental Science Center. (T. Marlowe, Interviewer, 2 December 2015.)

6 Exploring the contribution of National Parks to the entertainment industry's intellectual property

Thomas J. Liu, John B. Loomis, and Linda J. Bilmes

Introduction

'Want to visit Tatooine?' (the fictional desert planet featured in the original *Star Wars* movie), says the National Park Service (NPS) visitor's pamphlet and website for Death Valley National Park in California. The National Park System provides a guide for those who wish to retrace the steps of *Star Wars* movie characters R2-D2 and C3PO that were filmed in Death Valley NP. This is just one example of the use of NPS protected areas that are used in movies produced by the USA and other countries around the world. Yet most commonly used frameworks for valuing protected areas often overlook this value. With special effects and other cutting edge technology, filmmakers can create a plethora of scenarios including tornadoes and aliens. But when it comes to a natural setting, it is nearly impossible to replicate the untouched landscapes or iconic landmarks afforded by National Park Service units (NPS units). This chapter categorizes the types of value that protected iconic landmarks and landscapes provide to the film and TV industry and presents a methodology for estimating their economic contribution.

Understanding the contribution of NPS units to the production of movies and TV shows is important because the overall national production of movies and TV shows contributed nearly $100 billion to U.S. GDP in 2015. The movies and television sector accounts for nearly $1 of every $100 of U.S. GDP. Even this substantial figure understates the industry's importance as film production is one of America's greatest exports both monetarily, and in terms of the image of America presented globally. Part of that cultural influence includes memorable scenes from movies that have involved iconic shots of America including well-known sites within NPS units. In this chapter, we begin by categorizing how NPS units are used in movies and TV shows. We then provide methods by which one could value in dollar terms, the contribution of an NPS unit to a movie or TV show.

There are dozens of inputs that when combined create this $100 billion value industry, including the contributions of writers, actors, actresses, directors, producers, camera operators, and dozens (even hundreds, depending on the project) of support staff. For many movies that have one or more scenes shot outdoors, location scouts must find areas that meet the requirements of the writers and directors. NPS units (including National Parks, National Monuments, Historic Sites, etc.) play important yet often overlooked roles in television and movie industry. NPS units provide the following types of contributions to the film industry, all at a very low nominal cost to the production team:

1   Instantly recognizable iconic images in films (e.g., Washington Monument and Lincoln Memorial in Washington DC; Statue of Liberty in New York);
2   Grand untouched scenery that can serve as a world we know in an earlier time period (e.g., *Butch Cassidy and the Sundance Kid* in Zion NP; *Dances with Wolves* at Badlands NP) or other entirely different worlds (e.g., *Star Wars* at Death Valley NP);
3   'Thirty Mile Zone' (TMZ) around Hollywood, California, which includes the frequently used NPS unit, Santa Monica National Recreation Area.

Our summary analysis indicates that from the founding of the NPS in 1916 to 2013, the latest year of available data, at least 422 movies and TV shows have had one or more scenes filmed in units of the NPS. Most likely this is a substantial underestimate since each NPS unit independently issues its own permits for filming[1]. The NPS has not cataloged all these permits over the decades of filming. Even if NPS had cataloged all the permits, the permits are often issued to generic filming companies (e.g., 'XYZ Company'), which do not report the titles of the movie or TV program that it is filming. Therefore, there appears to be no complete centralized listing of names of movies and TV programs filmed across the 418 NPS units. As a result, this chapter lists the most well-known movies and TV shows filmed in NPS units to give the reader a sense of the role NPS units have played in top movies and TV shows of their day.

We first provide a synopsis of a sample of movies and TV shows filmed in each of the three categories listed. Many of the movies highlighted were big hit movies often referred to as 'blockbusters' and generated several billion in profits for film companies. While only a small percentage of that is attributable to the iconic settings or monuments provided by NPS units at minimal cost to the movie and TV studios, a small percentage of several billion dollars is a substantial value contributed by NPS units.

We then explore methods to estimate the economic contribution of NPS as input into the production of movies and TV shows. The orders of magnitude difference between the profits earned by movies, parts of which are shot in NPS units, and cost of NPS permits illustrates that there is a substantial economic benefit realized by the industry from access to NPS units. Thus, NPS units contribute to the value of the resulting intellectual property of the movie studio or TV industry. This value that the NPS units provide has been rarely studied from an economic perspective. This chapter makes a substantial contribution that we hope will stimulate further research in this area.

Summary of the NPS permitting process for filming movies and TV in NPS units

One way to count movies and TV shows filmed throughout the National Park System is to examine a subset of the permits issued by the NPS units. Each Park unit maintains its own permitting system, and the process varies to some extent by NPS unit. The typical permitting process is as follows: First, the requester fills out a one-to-four-page permit application, which includes a description of the proposal. The NPS unit then determines whether the filming proposal is consistent with the unit's mission, laws, and regulations. Typically the NPS unit quickly approves the permit if an area has been used for filming in the past. For more complex cases, an interdisciplinary NPS team of scientists and administrators meets to determine whether the permit should be approved. In some cases, an environmental analysis is performed. Once the proposal has been reviewed and pre- and post-filming mitigation measures (e.g., protecting certain areas from crews; post filming clean-up and restoration), the NPS unit signs off on it and issues a permit to film.

Although fees vary slightly by NPS unit, in general fees are typically charged on a daily basis and range from $150 per day to $750 per day as of August 2018[2], depending on the number of people involved in the filming. Additionally, the NPS unit often performs cost recovery for the cost of processing the permit and employees who monitor the production. If the production is large, monitors are hired to oversee the film crew to ensure that compliance with the permit is achieved. While these fees vary, the NPS unit does not obtain any 'profit' from the filming as the fees merely support the salary of the monitors.

Films incorporating iconic places

NPS units provide recognizable symbols or iconic images that often immediately provide important context to a movie scene. For example, the Washington Monument associates the scene with Washington DC, and the Statue of Liberty associates the scene with New York City. Beyond simply setting the location, the added value of providing this iconic image may also depend on the importance or memorability of the scene to the film as a whole. Thus, it is clear that the value contributed from the NPS unit is non-negligible. Further reinforcing this fact is that there are no substitutes for iconic resources such as the Statue of Liberty, the Lincoln Memorial, or Mount Rushmore. These locations are one of a kind places. This lack of substitutes increases the value that the NPS unit provides to a film or TV show.

Below are brief descriptions of a few movies filmed at iconic NPS units. Note that some of these films were not shot in the actual park site and instead feature the likeness of an iconic image preserved by an NPS unit. Although the value derived may be less than if that scene had been filmed at the actual site, these iconic images indicate that they contributed some value to the movie in their ability to provide an instantaneous conveyance of location or context to the viewer.

Forrest Gump—The National Mall (Lincoln Memorial)

This 1994 Oscar-winning movie portrays a kind-hearted Alabama man with a below-average IQ named Forrest Gump (played by screen star Tom Hanks). Forrest witnesses several key moments of American history during the presidencies of Kennedy and Johnson, with emphasis on the Vietnam War. During much of his adulthood Forrest often thinks of his childhood sweetheart, Jenny Curran. One of the pivotal scenes in this movie occurs when Forrest is attending a rally at the Lincoln Memorial in Washington DC and spots Jenny in the audience. Their joyful reunion splashing in the Reflecting Pool is one of the more memorable scenes of the movie.

Thelma & Louise—Canyonlands, Grand Canyon NP

In this 1991 Oscar-winning movie, two friends (played by screen stars Susan Sarandon and Geena Davis) are on a road trip. Their adventure turns into a race from the law after Louise kills a man who had tried to assault Thelma. In the closing scene, Thelma and Louise decide to launch themselves over the rim of the Grand Canyon in their '66 Thunderbird convertible rather than surrender to the police. While that the fatal plunge was filmed on U.S. Bureau of Land Management land near Moab, Utah, the movie suggests that the pair drive off the rim of Grand Canyon NP. It is this pivotal final scene that enshrines the movie in pop culture.

North by Northwest—Mt. Rushmore National Memorial

This 1959 classic movie was nominated for three Academy Awards and was directed by the legendary director Alfred Hitchcock. In this movie, gangsters mistake New York executive Roger Thornhill (played by a major star of that era, Cary Grant) for a government agent. They attempt to kill him, chasing him through Chicago, the Midwest, and to South Dakota. The final chase scene is filmed at Mount Rushmore NM in South Dakota.

*Close Encounters of the Third Kind—Devils Tower National
Monument*

The theme of the movie is a close encounter with a UFO that Roy Neary
(played by the star Richard Dreyfuss) and others have seen. They become
preoccupied by this close encounter. The storyline follows Roy as he keeps
imagining a strange towering mountain so much that he starts carving it
out of mud in the living room of his home. Then he sees an image of Devils
Tower broadcast on his TV set and realizes this is the place he has been
imagining. Soon he and many others are racing toward Devils Tower believ-
ing this is where the aliens will land. Roy Neary manages to elude several
attempts to prevent him from finding what turns out to be a UFO landing
site. Once there he initially sees several small space ships arrive. After these
small ships depart, an enormous 'mother ship' larger than Devils Tower
itself arrives. The use of Devils Tower as a size reference point gives the
viewer a sense of just how large the mothership is. Devils Tower NM is used
as a landmark in the film and features prominently in many scenes. We will
use this movie to illustrate one method of valuation of the contribution of
the Devils Tower to the movie.

Table 6.1 summarizes a more complete (but not exhaustive) list of famous
movies where one or more scenes were shot in an NPS unit and/or dialog
that the movie says is located in that NPS unit.

Films showing grand natural scenery or images

NPS units also provide a more subtle starring role in many blockbusters by
supplying awe-inspiring backdrops that even the most advanced computer-
generated technology cannot quite replicate. In fact, some parks are so dra-
matic that they are often used in sci-fi films as alien planets (*Star Wars*)
or prehistoric environments (*Jurassic Park*). Other NPS units offer pristine
environments that provide scenes that have remained largely untouched by
major development for nearly a century. As such they make ideal settings
to transport the viewer back to the Old West (*Butch Cassidy and Sundance
Kid*) or the early 1900s (Indiana Jones). Below we provide a brief description of a sample of NPS units that featured in major movies.

*Star Wars Episode IV: A New Hope and Star Wars VI: Return of the
Jedi—Death Valley National Park*

Star Wars remains one of the most successful movie franchises ever made.
Star Wars VI: Return of the Jedi was for many years the highest grossing
movie of all time and in inflation-adjusted dollars is still estimated to be in
the top five films of all time. While many of the movie's desert scenes were
filmed abroad in Tunisia, several key moments and transitional shots took
place in Death Valley NP[3]. For example, Mesquite Flats in Death Valley NP

Table 6.1 Examples of major motion pictures with iconic features and NPS unit filmed at or represented in the movie

Name of film	NPS unit	Year	Famous actors/actresses
National Treasure: Book of Secrets	Mt. Rushmore	2007	Nicolas Cage
Artificial Intelligence	Statue of Liberty	2001	Haley Joel Osment, Jude Law
X-Men	Statue of Liberty	2000	Patrick Stewart, Hugh Jackman, Ian McKellen
Titanic	Statue of Liberty	1997	Leonardo DiCaprio, Kate Winslet
The Rock	Golden Gate	1996	Sean Connery, Nicolas Cage, Ed Harris
Batman Forever	Statue of Liberty	1995	Val Kilmer, Tommy Lee Jones, Jim Carrey
Forrest Gump	Lincoln Memorial	1994	Tom Hanks, Robin Wright
Thelma & Louise	Canyonlands, Grand Canyon	1991	Susan Sarandon, Geena Davis, Brad Pitt
Ghostbusters II	Statue of Liberty	1989	Bill Murray, Dan Aykroyd, Sigourney Weaver
National Lampoon's Vacation	Grand Canyon	1983	Chevy Chase
Escape from New York	Statue of Liberty	1981	Kurt Russell
Superman II	Mt Rushmore	1980	Gene Hackman, Christopher Reeves
Close Encounters of the Third Kind	Devils Tower	1977	Richard Dreyfuss
Godfather Part II	Ellis Island	1974	Al Pacino, Robert De Niro, Robert Duvall
Planet of the Apes	Statue of Liberty, Lincoln Memorial	1968	Charlton Heston
North by Northwest	Mt. Rushmore	1959	Cary Grant, Eva Marie Saint
Mr. Smith Goes to Washington	Lincoln Memorial	1939	James 'Jimmy' Stewart

was where the robot named R2-D2 and a humanoid robot character named C3PO had their spat after crashing on Tatooine. The Artist's Palette area of Death Valley NP was where R2D2 was kidnapped.

Butch Cassidy and the Sundance Kid—Zion National Park

In this 1969 'western' movie that won four Academy Awards and was selected for preservation in the National Film Registry by the Library of Congress, Butch Cassidy (played by film star Paul Newman) and the Sundance Kid (played by film star Robert Redford) are two train robbers on the run from the law. They are going through areas of wilderness on horseback to avoid being captured. Much of the movie was filmed at or around Zion NP amongst its canyons. The park's wild landscape of sandstone cliffs, narrow canyons, arid grasslands, and forest provided a classic western backdrop as the film's two outlaws flee a posse determined to kill them.

Indiana Jones and the Last Crusade—Arches National Park

In this blockbuster 1989 movie, film star Harrison Ford plays Indiana Jones, an archaeologist who is searching for the Holy Grail (a cup used by Jesus Christ at the Last Supper and which received Christ's blood at the Cross). The opening sequence features a young Indiana Jones as a Boy Scout on horseback in the desert, heading towards what is Double Arch at Arches NP. This scenery is particularly relevant because immediately the viewer realizes that the young Indiana Jones is in a wild place, providing the scenery stunning enough for the beginning of this blockbuster movie.

Dances With Wolves—Badlands National Park

This 1990 movie is about a Civil War soldier played by film star Kevin Costner. He develops a relationship with a band of Lakota Indians and eventually joins them. Camera crews filmed several movie scenes at the mixed-grass prairie landscape they found at Badlands NP in southwestern South Dakota.

Jurassic Park: The Lost World—Redwood National Park

The Lost World is a 1997 movie about genetically engineered dinosaurs that escape and terrorize humans. Many of the forest scenes are filmed in Redwood National Park.

Table 6.2 provides a summary of these and many other (but not all) movies shot in NPS units because of their natural scenery.

Films and TV Shows at Santa Monica Mountains National Recreation Area within Hollywood's Key TMZ

Description of the TMZ

In many ways, Hollywood is synonymous with entertainment – many use it interchangeably when referring to the movie and TV industry. Although Hollywood is by definition a neighborhood and postal zip code within Los Angeles, California for those that work in the entertainment industry, 'Hollywood' means the 'Thirty Mile Zone' (or more infamously, the 'TMZ,'

Table 6.2 Sample of movies that used grand natural places of NPS units

Film	NPS unit	Year	Famous actors/actresses
Into the Wild	Denali NP	2007	Emile Hirsch, Vince Vaughn
Brokeback Mountain	Grand Teton NP	2005	Jake Gyllenhaal, Heath Ledger
Jurassic Park	Redwood NP	1993	Sam Neill, Laura Dern, Jeff Goldblum
Dances with Wolves	Badlands NP	1990	Kevin Costner
Indiana Jones and the Last Crusade	Arches NP	1989	Harrison Ford, Sean Connery
Star Trek V	El Capitan at Yosemite NP	1989	William Shatner, Leonard Nimoy
Rocky IV (snow training scenes)	Grand Teton NP	1985	Sylvester Stallone, Talia Shire
ET	Redwood NP	1982	Henry Thomas, Drew Barrymore
The Shining	Glacier NP	1980	Jack Nicholson, Shelley Duvall
Star Wars (desert scenes)	Death Valley NP	1977	Mark Hamill, Harrison Ford, Carrie Fisher
The Eiger Sanction	Grand Teton NP	1975	Clint Eastwood
Butch Cassidy and the Sundance Kid	Zion NP	1969	Paul Newman, Robert Redford
Greatest Story Ever Told	Arches NP, Death Valley NP, Canyonlands NP	1965	Max von Sydow, Dorothy McGuire, Charlton Heston

which is also the name of a celebrity gossip company). While the exact boundaries have changed through the decades, today, the zone extends over a 30-mile radius and pivots around the intersection of La Cienega and Beverly boulevards[4].

Why the TMZ matters

This TMZ has consequences for studios and workers in the entertainment industry. Virtually all the workers involved with movie and TV production are union members[5]. The entertainment industry and labor unions use the TMZ studio zone to determine work rules and compensation for union workers in the film industry. Within the boundaries of the TMZ, projects are considered 'local' and on-set laborers, particularly extras and other craftspeople, are expected to transport themselves; the zone also determines pay scales and other working conditions. Workers outside the zone are considered 'on location' and the studios become responsible for transportation, meals, hotels, and additional compensation. Therefore shooting within the TMZ means saving on cost to the movie and TV studios.

The other advantage of staying within the TMZ is the availability of the wide variety of labor and other inputs that are required to produce a movie or TV show. A movie requires an enormous variety of worker skills and support service inputs (e.g., stage prop construction, make-up, etc.). The TMZ is one of the few places that has the required concentration of these needed services.

The role of the NPS units in the TMZ

One of the few remaining areas within the TMZ that is not crisscrossed with streets and development is the Santa Monica Mountains National Recreation Area (NRA). Thus it is one of the few sources of untouched scenery within the TMZ. This makes the Santa Monica Mountains NRA a popular place to film movies and TV shows. In 2012, 43 films and television show episodes were filmed in the TMZ. These episodes included *The Biggest Loser, Modern Family, America's Most Wanted, Millionaire Matchmaker*, and *The Good Wife*. The Santa Monica Mountains NRA also contains the Paramount Ranch, which was originally owned by Paramount Studios and used for decades for filming. Paramount Ranch was used from 1992 to 1997 to film the TV show *Dr. Quinn, Medicine Woman*.[6] There are several cost savings of staying within the TMZ: (a) labor travel time costs to studios and workers themselves; (b) transportation cost savings of driving or flying to other more distant locations. Such cost savings are often particularly important for single TV episodes without large budgets.

The importance of the Paramount Ranch is indicated by the entertainment industry's rapid response to the loss of this area and surrounding areas of Santa Monica Mountains NRA due to the massive Woosley Fire during November 2018. The industry plans to rebuild the Paramount Ranch prior to 2021 with consultation from Hollywood experts, historians, architects, and the public.

What follows is a short description of a popular TV show filmed at the Santa Monica Mountains NRA. Following this is Table 6.3, which provides a more comprehensive, but not exhaustive, list of shows.

M*A*S*H TV series

Some hit TV series such as *M*A*S*H*, 1972–1983, starring among others Alan Alda, were shot in Malibu Creek State Park. This State Park is one of the three collaborating California State Parks lying within the Santa Monica Mountains NRA. The land where the show was shot originally belonged to 20th Century Fox studios. The relics of the *M*A*S*H* TV series have been restored in honor of its 25th anniversary. These are now in much their original condition and location when the series was shot there. The sitcom featuring the U.S. Army during the Korean War and the doctors and nurses at a mobile Army surgical hospital (hence the initials M*A*S*H) received over 100 Emmy nominations during its 11 seasons.[7]

Table 6.3 Examples of movies and TV shows with scenes shot in Santa Monica Mountains NRA TMZ

Film	Year(s)	Famous Actors/Actresses
American Sniper	2014	Bradley Cooper, Sienna Miller
Inception	2010	Leonardo DiCaprio
Race to Witch Mountain	2009	Dwayne 'The Rock' Johnson
The Bucket List	2007	Jack Nicholson, Morgan Freeman
Norbit	2006	Eddie Murphy
The Lake House	2006	Keanu Reeves, Sandra Bullock
Letters from Iwo Jima	2006	Ken Watanabe
Memoirs of a Geisha	2005	Gong Li, Zhang Ziyi, Ken Watanabe
The Girl Next Door	2004	Emile Hirsch, Elisha Cuthbert
Van Helsing	2003	Hugh Jackman, Kate Beckinsale
Windtalkers	2002	Nicolas Cage, Adam Beach
Flintstones in Viva Rock Vegas	2000	Mark Addy, Stephen Baldwin
Blast from the Past	1999	Brendan Fraser, Alicia Silverstone
The Great Outdoors	1988	Dan Aykroyd, John Candy
Wisdom	1986	Emilio Estevez, Demi Moor, Tom Skerritt
House II: The Second Story	1984	Arye Gross, Lar Park Lincoln
Reds	1981	Warren Beatty, Diane Keaton, Jack Nicholson
Dr. Quinn, Medicine Woman (TV)	1993–1998	Jane Seymour, Joe Lando
*M*A*S*H* (TV)	1972–1983	Alan Alda, Mike Ferrell, Loretta Swit
The Biggest Loser (TV)	2004–2016	Alison Sweeney, Jillian Michaels, Bob Harper

Methods for Valuing the Contribution of NPS units to Movies & Television

The first step in the economic valuation of movies and TV shows set in NPS units is to collect data on revenues and production costs. This information for movies can often be obtained from the Internet Movie Database (IMDb, www.imdb.com).

Searching for the movie name, and scrolling down to the category 'Box Office' provides information on the revenue movies gross both in the USA and cumulatively worldwide. Additionally, in the same 'Box Office' category the budget to make the movie is provided. Once both the gross revenues and the production costs are updated for inflation, and advertising costs deducted, the profit from the movie can be calculated. Table 6.4 provides estimates of the profits made by each movie in the three categories we have examined.

We want to decompose this profit measure to determine which parts can be in some way be attributed to the movie's use of the NPS units either in terms of scenery, iconic symbol or location. There are two methods that can

Table 6.4 Profits associated with movies that included a scene or image from an NPS unit (Billions $2015)

Movie category	Total revenue[a]	Total production cost w/out advertising	Total movie cost with advertising[b]	Profits earned	Examples
Use of iconic NPS units	$14.130	$1.686	$2.428	$11.701	*Forrest Gump, North by Northwest*
Use of grand scenery NPS units	$17.333	$0.774	$1.115	$16.218	*Star Wars, ET, Close Encounters of the Third Kind*
Use of Santa Monica Mtn NRA TMZ	$3.158	$1.265	$1.822	$1.336[c]	*The Bucket List, Great Outdoors*

a   Includes revenue both U.S. and worldwide if distributed globally, as well as any DVD sales.
b   Soloviechik (2014: 22) indicates that using movie data from 1915 to 2010, that advertising averaged 44% of the film production costs.
c   Does not include TV shows, which generate profits via commercials on shows, and movies for which no budget information was provided in IMDB.com.

be used to estimate the economic values that NPS units provide movie and TV industry. First is *residual imputation.* This has been widely used to estimate the value attributable to unpriced or underpriced inputs provided by governments for decades. Examples include government-provided irrigation water (Young and Loomis, 2014) and grazing lands, which have a value to the farmers and public land ranchers, respectively, far in excess to what the government agencies charge the producer for these resources.

The number of scenes or the amount of time the movie shows that scenery or iconic image might be a rough indicator of the 'amount of NPS unit' input used in making the movie itself. However, these approximations measuring the quantity of the NPS unit used might understate the contribution of some well-known iconic NPS units whose geographic location is so well known that using that image is a 'short cut' by the director to quickly convey location of the scene (e.g., Statue of Liberty with New York City, Lincoln Memorial in Washington DC). Despite this potential shortcoming, the residual imputation method holds significant promise to value NPS units used in movies. Below this approach is described in more detail, along with an illustration using the movie *Close Encounters of the Third Kind* to value the contribution of Devils Tower National Monument.

The second method is *cost savings* to the movie and TV industry. For illustrative purposes, we use the TMZ. The accounting cost savings are straight forward enough to calculate for production of movies and TV shows. Specifically one would compare the costs to film within the TMZ and outside the TMZ. This would involve added costs of travel, lodging, per diem, etc. However, determining the full economic cost is a more complicated exercise as we would need to consider the costs to find alternatives to filming locations, that is, the costs involved in filming elsewhere. This cost measurement could include time spent to search for alternative locations, fees paid for use of private land, travel time, etc. Along with formal cost accounting, this presents a realistic value of the total savings afforded the film and television industry for using the TMZ.

Additional economic cost savings from operating within the TMZ include the close proximity to the necessary skilled workers. There are not only accounting cost savings to the industry, but also the reduced travel cost in terms of time to workers who can travel from home to the set daily. Both of these economic cost savings are often measured by economists using the wage rate (Parsons, 2017). There are also transportation cost savings in terms of fuel, and associated air pollution and climate change damages from added travel whether by car/truck and/or plane if more distant travel was required to find suitable filming locations. The transportation and lodging cost savings can potentially be estimated by identifying the alternative location that would be used for filming if the TMZ area were unavailable. For example, if locations within the Santa Monica Mountains NRA, which are within the TMZ, substitute for a shooting location outside the TMZ, the average cost savings to the studio is $1.118 million per location (Soloveichik, 2013)[8]. This is a significant cost savings to the studio. The same thought process would be required to think about what the substitute locations might be for other NPS units that provide iconic images or untouched scenery.

Details of residual imputation of movie profit to NPS units

The underlying concept of the residual imputation method is that the value an unpriced or underpriced input (NPS unit) can be calculated by taking the difference total revenue (e.g., a movie's gross) and subtracting out the costs of all the market inputs, where costs include a 'normal' return to the studio. The amount left over is the 'residual' that can be interpreted as the maximum amount a company would pay to use the unpriced or underpriced input, e.g., the NPS unit. However, there may be other underpriced inputs used in movies since many cities, states or countries charge very little to use their iconic images (e.g. a New York City filming permit costs $300 and provides access to a wide variety of landmarks such as the Empire State Building, Times Square, Brooklyn Bridge, NY subway; Central Park in NYC does not charge a fee but asks for a donation[9]). More than half the states in the USA[10] and dozens of countries subsidize movie production via tax credits on qualifying movies. Thus if a movie 'grosses' $10 million, and the cost of all the market-priced inputs is $9 million, then there is $1 million in residual value to be split up among the other underpriced inputs such as movie locations. In the following section, we provide an example of how to apportion part of that value to the NPS units using the movie *Close Encounters of the Third Kind*.

Short cut method to estimating the profit attributable to the contribution of NPS unit iconic images or scenery

The most straightforward way to implement the residual imputation method is to start with the Internet Movie Database (www.imdb.com). There the website reports the Gross USA and 'Cumulative Worldwide Gross', which is the total with worldwide revenue (occasionally DVD sales listed as well). The 'Box Office' section also provides an estimated budget. Since this budget is presumably the production budget, it would be necessary to account for advertising. The U.S. Bureau of Economic Analysis statistical analysis (Soloveichik, 2014: 22) suggests multiplying by the budget by the 1.44 to account for the additional 44% spent on advertising. Follows (2016) suggests 30% is advertising (so 1.33). There is also studio overhead for setting up and running the studio's office. This includes the legal staff to write contracts, accountants, and staff to sort through the hundreds of potential movie manuscripts submitted to the studio (Soloveichik, 2014). Follows (2016) estimates this to be around 15%[11].

In performing a residual imputation analysis, economists allow for a 'normal' rate of return on the money (i.e., capital) tied up in producing and advertising the movie. Determining what is a 'normal rate of return' to the studio and production company is difficult. There is always an 'opportunity cost' of the foregone rate of return to funds invested in any productive enterprise. For example, rather than invest their money in a risky movie production, a studio or producer could invest in U.S. Treasury Notes, which are a risk-free investment, earning say 4%. In some circumstances, the smaller studios may actually have to borrow some or all the money to make the film that then becomes a real financing cost that is charged to the movie by the studios, so the normal rate of profit would be above and beyond this financing cost.

Part of the normal rate of return is the compensation for the risk taking associated with potentially not recouping that money if the movie does poorly at the theaters. In terms of risk, upfront investment of tens of millions of dollars in movies is certainly a risky investment. Many movies never make it to the theaters and go straight to premium channels such as HBO, or to DVDs and streaming because test audiences or initial reviews indicate it is not worth spending the additional nearly 30–44% more to advertise and market the movie. The likelihood of loss is substantial as only half the movies made a monetary profit after all the costs we have described so far, including any financing have been accounted for (Follows, 2016[12]). Thus, the payment for this higher risk (sometimes called a risk premium) also needs to be factored in to the costs.

Using data for 29 movies produced from 2005 to 2015 with a production budget of over $100 million, Follows (2016) yields an average rate of return of 3.7% after financing costs. The amount left over after all costs including the 3.7% normal profit would be considered an economic profit, and hence the residual that might be attributed to all underpriced or unpriced resources including the NPS unit.

How much of this residual might be attributable to NPS unit locational resources? There are often a dozen locations used in filming. Some of these charge minimal costs to use their location. According to Simon and Weise (2006: 55), some locations charge as little as $1, others a few thousand dollars a day. As noted above some cities, states and countries charge a minimal amount or even subsidize movie production companies through tax credits to come film. *The key is that the total residual value should be split up such as that all underpriced scenery or iconic images receive value in proportion to their use or significance in the movie in such a way that all that exhausts or uses up this residual*[13].

The quantity of unpriced or underpriced locations can be measured in many different ways. One is the number of scenes where the NPS unit's image and other unpriced/underpriced images are shown. Another is that the quantity of NPS input could be approximated by the amount of time the NPS unit and other unpriced/underpriced images are shown in the movie. We recognize both of these are imperfect measures, but these are observable and objective measures. Another measure might be the 'importance' of the NPS unit to the movie (e.g., a climactic scene). However, determination requires a degree of subjectivity involving reviewing movie critics' evaluation of the movie for hints regarding the role the NPS unit played in the film. Given the limitations associated with each measure, it may be important to not only report the monetary valuation using an objective measure but supplement that with a qualitative description of the role the NPS unit contributes to the film. In this way a more complete sense of the value the NPS unit contributed to the movie's value can be assessed.

Empirical example of short cut residual imputation using Close Encounters of the Third Kind

This 1977 movie that stars Richard Dreyfuss was summarized earlier in this chapter. From IMDB we find that worldwide gross revenue is $303,788,635, which when updated for inflation is $1.188 billion.

IMDB states that production costs (in 1977) were estimated at $20 million, which when updated for inflation amount to $78.2 million. Accounting for advertising brings up the cost to $112.61 million. Adding 15% for studio overhead results in a total cost of $129.5 million. Accounting for the normal or average rate of return of 3.7% the resulting excess or economic profit is $1.02 billion. What is not known is how much of this profit may have been paid to actors/actresses or the director as profit sharing. Thus, the

$1 billion is the maximum residual that can be allocated to all the under-priced or unpriced resources.

The movie scenes featuring Devils Tower National Monument are on the screen for a total of six minutes. Given that the movie is 135 minutes long, this accounts for 4.4% of the total running time. Applying this 4.4% to the $1.02 billion profit is $45 million as the value contributed by Devils Tower NM. This approach assumes that the value of Devils Tower NM to the movie is proportional to its 'screen time'. This assumption may understate the value that freestanding Devils Tower NM contributes to the movie. Specifically, there are limited substitutes in the USA (outside of other NPS units) that could represent a monolith of such magnitude that it served the two purposes of the movie: (a) plausibly acting as a landmark for alien spacecraft; (b) to illustrate the relative size of the alien spacecraft. This reinforces the importance of providing a qualitative description of the importance of the NPS unit when presenting estimates of the economic value of NPS units used in movies.

Details of the theory underlying the residual imputation method

In this section, we first review the conceptual foundation of the residual imputation method. This is followed by providing an empirical specification of this method for movies. The estimates we will provide in the following equations are for those situations where reliable data from IMDB or elsewhere are not available.

Equation 1 provides the adaptation of the basic formula for residual imputation to movies. Y represents the quantity of output and p_y is the price per unit of output. In this case, we have data for $Y \times p_y$, which is the movie's gross revenue including the worldwide revenue if the movie played overseas, as well as any DVD sales and streaming revenues. Q_i represents the quantity of any given input i while P_i are the prices of inputs i.

$$Y \times p_y = P_a \times Q_a + P_w \times Q_w + P_l \times Q_l + P_{SE} \times Q_{SE}$$
$$+ P_{prod} \times Q_{prod} + P_{AD} \times Q_{AD} + P_{mfg} \times Q_{mfg} \qquad (1)$$
$$+ RR + Q_{ps}(\$) + P_{NPS} \times Q_{NPS} + P_{unp} \times Q_{unp}$$

Where:

$P_a \times Q_a$ = wage paid to actor times the number of hours worked where pay rates can vary depending on the actor;

$P_w \times Q_w$ = number of hours of nonactor workers, P_w is the price per worker in the same units as Q_w;

$P_l \times Q_l$ = the price times the cost of filming at each location;

$P_{SE} \times Q_{SE}$ = total cost of special effect companies;

$P_{prod} \times Q_{prod}$ = total cost of production level employees (producer, directors, etc.);

$P_{AD} \times Q_{AD}$ = total cost of advertising;

$P_{mfg} \times Q_{mfg}$ = manufacturing and distribution costs

RR = normal rate of return on capital invested (includes risk taken by producers);

$Q_{ps}(\$)$ = money involved in any profit-sharing arrangements;

$P_{NPS} \times Q_{NPS}$ = total value of the *NPS* included in the movie. Includes a number of scenes shot with the NPS unit or minutes the NPS scenery is shown. P is the implicit price for which we are trying to solve with the residual imputation method;

$P_{unp} \times Q_{unp}$ = underpriced total cost of subsidized locations.

Drawing on the U.S. Bureau of Economic Analysis (Soloveichik, 2014) multiple regression study of movies from 1915 to 2010 using detailed movie specific data, we have estimates of the cost per unit of input or price of many of these inputs for a typical film. To start with we use Soloveichik (2014) for prices. Applying some of her estimates we can model equation (2) from equation (1):

$$Y \times p_y = \left(\left(\$46 \times Q_a + \$172 \times Q_w + \$1,118 \times Q_l + \$4,448 \times Q_{SE} \right) * 1000 \right)$$
$$+ P_{prod} \times Q_{prod} + P_{AD} \times Q_{AD} + P_{mfg} \times Q_{mfg} + RR + Q_{ps} + P_{NPS} \times Q_{NPS} \quad (2)$$
$$+ P_{unp} \times Q_{unp}$$

Where we have specific prices for certain variables that are then multiplied to put the estimates in thousands $USD, e.g., 46 in the first line is $46,000.

Soloveichik (2014) includes producers in 'non-actor workers', so we will combine Q_{prod} into this variable to get equation (3). Unfortunately, IMDB does not include advertising data. However, Soloveichik (2014:22) indicates that movie studios spend about 44% of their filming budget on advertising. While she notes this is a substantial addition to total costs, she believes such a large expense may be justified by the revenues not only at the box office but in subsequent DVD sales and nowadays, streaming revenues. Mathematically this is represented by including a factor of 1.44 to the direct production costs, which can be seen in equation (3). Similarly, typical accounting conventions charge overhead as a percentage of the total cost. Thus overhead would apply to all of what are sometimes called direct costs. Any sharing of profits ($QPS) beyond the payment to the producers and studios to the lead actors and directors is a difficult variable to factor in. As Soloveichik (2014: 23) notes that in some sense this profit sharing is just an additional payment to actors and directors, so in principle it may be embedded in P_a and P_{prod}. Thus, Soloveichik (2014) did not include it in her multiple regression. Nonetheless, profit-sharing arrangements when they exist can pose a difficult challenge to the residual imputation method since, this method attempts to attribute some of the excess profits (what in movie jargon is actually called 'residuals') to the unpriced resource (here NPS unit iconic images or scenery). If in fact all the excess profit is already allocated to the actors and directors, there is little left over for the unpriced resource.

For our purposes of illustration, we will follow Soloveichik (2014) and omit any profit sharing. Thus accounting for the available data then, equation (2) becomes equation (3):

$$Y \times p_y = \left(\left(\left(46 \times Q_a + 172 \times Q_w + 1{,}118 \times Q_l + 4{,}448 \times Q_{SE}\right) * 1000\right)\right.$$
$$\left. * 1.44\right) * 1.15 + RR + P_{NPS} \times Q_{NPS} + P_{unp} \times Q_{unp} \tag{3}$$

Solving for the residual value (the unpriced NPS unit iconic images and/or scenery and other underpriced scenery):

$$P_{NPS} \times Q_{NPS} + P_{unp} \times Q_{unp} = Y \times p_y - \left(\left(\left(46 \times Q_a\right.\right.\right.$$
$$+ 172 \times Q_w + 1{,}118 \times Q_l + 4{,}448 \tag{4}$$
$$\left.\left.\left. \times Q_{SE}\right) * 1000\right) * 1.44\right) * 1.15 - RR$$

Equation 4 states that the potential residual value to the NPS unit and other underpriced or unpriced locations is equal to the *difference* between all of the movie revenue (box office, TV revenue, DVDs, etc.) and all the production cost, including 44% advertising (the 1.44) and 15% overhead (the 1.15) and a normal rate of return (RR—about 3.7% as noted by Follows (2016)) to the movie producer and movie studio.

To operationalize equation (4), the quantity of inputs used in any particular movie is needed. There are two sources for this information. If the movie is listed in IMDB then the quantity of many of these inputs can be found. The number of actors, the number of crew, and special effects companies associated with a movie can all be accessed from the IMDB site for a given film.

If the movie is not listed in IMDB, then Simon and Wiese (2006: 221–269) provide a typical budget for a $5 million film budget. In their budget, they provide the price per unit for a large number of specialties as well and the typical quantity that would be used. Some of the variable costs in Simon and Wiese's $5 million budget could be scaled up and down to more expensive and less expensive movies by varying the quantities. These authors also provide a dataset of standard budgets (2006: 220). Follows (2014) provides estimates of the average number of crew and provides estimates for a variety of specialties of the top 1,000 files from 1994 to 2013, making it more current than Simon and Wiese (2006).

Once the right-hand side of equation (4) has been calculated then the amount remaining (i.e., the residual) should, if all other costs have been accurately estimated, represent the maximum value of all the NPS unit's contribution plus that of the other unpriced and underpriced locations. This residual value then needs to be apportioned or allocated across the various unpriced or underpriced inputs (e.g., locations) in such a manner that reflects the contribution. As we noted earlier, this could be done using minutes or the number of scenes the particular location or unpriced input is used in the movie or even a more subjective measure of importance could be appropriate given the circumstance. Whatever metric or approach used, the total residual is the upper bound of the total value contributed by the NPS unit and other unpriced inputs.

Uncertainty arises in the residual imputation method when determining whether all other market priced inputs have been accurately estimated. When possible one can rely on film specific costs. Doing this increases the likelihood that the estimate of the residual associated with the NPS unit and other unpriced or underpriced is accurate. Since it is not always possible to find all inputs used in specific movies, or there is a judgment call involved when some movie-specific inputs are missing, it is best to provide a range of input values. This will provide a range of values for the residual, and therefore a range in the portion of the residual value associated with the NPS unit(s) used in the movie. Such a range is still quite informative. Such a range is likely to be more credible to decision makers than a single number anyway. Most decision makers may correctly sense that a single precise value of the NPS unit's contribution to a particular movie is unlikely to be very accurate. While the range in monetary estimates of the contribution of the NPS unit to the movie is the quantitative information, including the narrative about how the context the NPS unit was used in the movie is also informative. This qualitative information helps the decision maker to assess whether the quantitative valuation information is likely to be an underestimate or not.

Sometimes it is informative to explicitly report that one more minute or one more scene with an NPS unit contributed $X. This is the 'implicit' price or shadow price of another unit of NPS location. For example, if one has measured Q_{NPS} in minutes, then this would be the 'value' of another minute of time the NPS unit is shown in the movie. If Q_{NPS} is measured by the number of scenes, then the 'value' is for another scene where the NPS unit is shown. These value estimates can be informative, but caution is needed in taking too much away from these per unit estimates. They are primarily accurate within the context of that particular movie. Only if one had these estimates for dozens of movies would one be able to make overall inferences about the value of NPS units in movies. Once again it is important to supplement such a statement about the relative value of another NPS unit location with the qualitative contribution that the NPS unit made to the movie, which could vary especially if used for example in a climactic scene of the movie.

It is worth noting that if the price or quantity of all market inputs are overestimated, then the residual associated with the unpriced input (e.g. NPS unit) will be understated or could even appear negative. As noted previously, Fellows (2016) found that of the 30 recent major ($100 million-plus budget) movies that half of them made money and half of them lost money, at least as he noted on paper (but as Fellows also noted, studios have an interest in inflating costs—see endnote 12). As such, the residual value could be negative, suggesting that no return whatsoever to the unpriced or underpriced inputs. In these cases, a qualitative assessment of how the NPS unit was used in the movie may be more useful. More details on the residual implementation method can be found in Young and Loomis (2014).

Conclusion

National Parks, National Recreation Areas, and Monuments provide protected landscapes and iconic images that film makers and TV shows have drawn upon for decades. These iconic images are used in a variety of ways, whether it be to evoke the wonders of a serene untouched wilderness or to quickly signal a specific location in a busy metropolis to audiences. The varied natural landscapes of NPS units provide an ability to transport the viewer to time periods before the settlement of the west or provide the appearances of otherworldly places. Our review of movies and TV shows that have filmed one or more scenes in NPS units estimates that these have earned roughly $29 billion in profits (see Table 6.4). While the incremental contribution of the NPS units is only a small portion of this amount, in absolute terms, this is a sizeable amount. Yet the NPS receives very minimal payment for allowing filming in the NPS units. A methodology was presented and illustrated that allows for calculating the incremental value that NPS units provide to the film and TV industry. This methodology could equally be applied to nearly all public lands, whether State Parks, State Forests, or National Forests, as well as international parks. Whether the iconic image be the Eiffel Tower in Paris, the Matterhorn in Switzerland, a wildlife preserve in Kenya, or Mount Fuji in Japan, all these images or landscapes often make a material contribution to a film's revenues and profits otherwise they would not have been used. Society and government budget offices could use this methodology to help quantify the additional value that protecting these historic structures and iconic landscapes presents.

Acknowledgments

We would like to thank Kenneth Norris, Harvard University, for his edits to this chapter that have clarified several points.

Notes

1 As described later in this chapter, each NPS unit is responsible for issue its own permit to the movie or TV studio wishing to film one or more scenes in that NPS unit (see https://www.nps.gov/aboutus/news/commercial-film-and-photo-permit s.htm). Since the movies and TV shows filmed in NPS units date back decades, there appears to be no central registry of all the TV shows and movies filmed in NPS units.

2 https://www.nps.gov/aboutus/news/commercial-film-and-photo-permits.htm

3 See https://www.nps.gov/deva/planyourvisit/star-wars-in-death-valley.htm for a brief discussion of filming of Star Wars in Death Valley National Park.

4 For a map and more details see *https://www.kcet.org/shows/lost-la/studio-lab or-and-the-origins-of-hollywoods-thirty-mile-zone-or-tmz*

5 http://www.latimes.com/business/hollywood/la-fi-ct-hollywood-unions-20 170509-story.html

6 See https://www.nps.gov/samo/planyourvisit/paramountranch.htm for more details.

7 See http://www.malibucreekstatepark.org/MASH.html for more details, maps and photos.

8 See U.S. Bureau of Economic Analysis study of the average incremental cost of adding another filming location for a film by Soloveichik (2013).

9 See http://www.centralparknyc.org/visit/filming-and-photography.html

10 See The Hollywood Reporter for a listing of the various states and different forms these subsidies take, https://www.hollywoodreporter.com/news/film-t v-tax-incentives-a-885699

11 See http://marshallinside.usc.edu/mweinstein/teaching/fbe552/552secure/notes/ deal%20structures.pdf for an example from University of Southern California in Los Angeles which suggestions the overhead is 15%. This 15% seems low given the experience of this chapters' authors in other settings (e.g., universities and consulting firms).

12 Although Follows also notes that there is some tendency for studios to inflate costs to make movies look like they are making minimal profits on paper. This avoids them having to pay profit sharing to star actors. This of course tends to understate the residual to be allocated to underpriced or unpriced inputs such as NPs.

13 The logic of this rests on what economists call Euler's Theorem of product exhaustion across all the factors of production, including any unpriced or under-priced ones (Young and Loomis, 2014).

References

Follows, S. 2014. How Many People Work on a Hollywood Film? https://stephen follows.com/how-many-people-work-on-a-hollywood-film/.

Follows, S. 2016. How Movies Make Money: $100m+ Hollywood Blockbusters. https://stephenfollows.com/how-movies-make-money-hollywood-blockbusters/.

Parsons, G. 2017. Travel Cost Models. In P. Champ, K. Boyle, and T. Brown (Eds.). *A Primer on Nonmarket Valuation*, 2nd Edition. Dordrecht, The Netherlands: Springer, pp.187–234.

Simon, D. and M. Weise. 2006. *Film and Video Budgets*, 4th updated Edition. Studio City, CA: Michael Weise Productions.

Soloveichik, R. 2010. Artistic originals as a capital asset. *American Economic Review*, 100(2): 110–114.

Soloveichik, R. 2013. Theatrical Movies as Capital Assets. Unpublished paper. Washington, DC: U.S. Bureau of Economic Analysis.

Young, R. and J. Loomis. 2014. *Determining the Economic Value of Water*, 2nd Edition. New York, NY: RFF Press.

7 Benefits of National Park Service cooperative programs

Stephen R. Thompson, Linda J. Bilmes, and John B. Loomis

Introduction

This chapter investigates the economic value of National Park Service (NPS) programs that occur largely outside the boundaries of the National Park Service units (NPS units). This chapter illustrates that the benefits of the NPS extend far beyond the NPS units into the surrounding communities, many of which are not near NPS units. In particular, this chapter focuses on what the NPS calls its cooperative programming and collaborative partnerships throughout the USA. NPS cooperative programming can be grouped into four overall categories: education, historical preservation, conservation of natural environments of importance to communities, and improvement in local recreational opportunities. Many of these functions also have their counterparts at state and local governmental levels in partnership with national and grassroots conservation groups. These cooperative program relationships are also quite common internationally between multiple governmental agencies and international non-governmental organizations (NGOs), with the World Wildlife Fund as an example. Thus, the qualitative and quantitative valuation methods that are discussed in this chapter have applicability at the state and local level as well as globally.

Several of the elements of NPS cooperative programs have been briefly discussed in prior chapters. As was shown in Figure 1.1 in Chapter 1, the lower branch of the NPS is made up of cooperative programming and its many elements. Chapter 2 on the total economic value (TEV) of the NPS reported values of four groupings of the NPS programs based on results from a survey of U.S. households. The educational values of NPS programs were studied in-depth in Chapter 5.

In contrast, this chapter provides a more in-depth investigation of the NPS programs, with particular emphasis on the value of NPS collaborations. The chapter proposes methods for valuing individual elements of the main categories of NPS programs. This chapter also uses the NPS Chesapeake Bay Office, which operates entirely through cooperative programming and collaboration, as a case study. This case study illustrates how interviews can be used to qualitatively document the values of cooperative programming between stakeholders. In addition, the case study is used to provide an empirical example of one of the valuation methods proposed at the beginning of the chapter.

NPS programming is different than many traditional areas of the NPS, because (a) it is often a function performed outside of NPS boundaries, and (b) the NPS cannot claim full credit for the beneficial outcomes of these programs because they rely on effective partnerships. Thus, two questions must be answered: first, how can we define the value that is created from cooperative programming services that occur outside of parks and protected area? Second, how can we allocate and quantify the value of individual stakeholders operating collaboratively on joint projects? We propose answers to both. However, quantifying precisely how much value can be attributed to the NPS as a result of program outcomes is challenging because there is an element of what economists call 'joint production' in the multi-stakeholder production process. Nonetheless, we propose some alternative methods that might be considered to answer the second question.

Classifications and categories of NPS cooperative programs

It is necessary to provide a basic understanding of NPS programs prior to discussing their value. NPS programs account for a wide array of activities, including 'recreation planning, preservation of natural, cultural, and historic resources, and environmental compliance' (Department of the Interior, 2015, NR&P–1). They are central to federal recreation and preservation efforts, but also critical to cross-agency collaboration and coordination. NPS programming aligns federal and state policies and provides funding and technical expertise to federal, state, tribal, and local governments, as well as private and non-profit organizations.

Chapter 2 provided a broad categorization of the four types of NPS programs for the purposes of providing a concise summary for inclusion in the TEV survey. These four categories are listed here:

1 Preservation of local historic buildings and sites, which commemorate American history and culture or significant events and people.
2 Creation and improvement of recreation opportunities for communities.
3 Protection of natural environments and features that are important to communities.
4 Educational programs which help children and adults learn about historical, cultural, and environmental topics.

These broad categories represent dozens of individual programs that reach every corner of the USA and affect millions of people, many of whom never set foot in an NPS unit. Table 7.1 provides examples of the detailed programs of the NPS. The reader can find more details in National Park Service (2013b).

Table 7.1 Examples of NPS programs

Historic Site preservation
American Battlefield Protection Program
Heritage Documentation Program
Historic Lighthouse Preservation Program
Historic Preservation Tax Incentives Program
Maritime Heritage Initiative
National Heritage Areas Program

National Historic Landmarks Program
National Register of Historic Places
National Underground Railroad Network to Freedom Program

Historic Site management training
National Center for Preservation Technology and Training
National Native American Graves Protection and Repatriation Act (NAGPRA)
  Program

Recreation Lands
Federal Lands to Parks Program
Hydropower Recreation Assistance Program
Land and Water Conservation Fund State Assistance Program
National Trails System Program
National Wild and Scenic Rivers Program
Rivers, Trails, and Conservation Assistance Program

Despite the large number of NPS programs and the ubiquitous presence of many of the programs (e.g., there are 92,000 properties on the National Register of Historic Places[1] most of which are outside of NPS units), NPS programs make up just 1.7% of the total NPS budget. This minimal budget may be one contributing factor in why past studies have overlooked its value. As explored later, it is through leveraging this small amount of NPS budget with the personnel, budget, and resources of state and local groups that the NPS programs can have a significant impact throughout the USA. Importantly, the NPS programs play an important role in how the NPS fulfills its mission, particularly where there are significant natural and cultural resources in urban areas. It is through these urban areas that the NPS can reach new, diverse audiences and 'be relevant to all Americans' ('The Urban Agenda—Urban Parks and Programs (U.S. National Park Service)' 2016).

Choi and Marlowe (2012: 28–30) describe NPS programmatic services as a starting point to understand programmatic value. These programmatic services are:

- Funding
- Coordination and management
- Technical expertise
- Organizational leveraging.

These four programmatic services often represent the NPS's inputs that contribute to and enhance networks of local and state governments along with numerous NGOs. An empirical study of National Estuary Programs shows that government interventions using networks can be most effective if they transcend jurisdictional lines. For example, networks might span multiple levels of government ('vertical spanning'), local jurisdictions bordering each other geographically ('horizontal spanning'), various interest groups ('expertise spanning'), or stakeholders with different incentives and motives ('ideological spanning'). Initiatives that bridge multiple boundaries were most effective, with positive outcomes in terms of developing trust and cooperation—even among partners with competing interests (Schneider et al., 2003). This trust is important: without it, there is evidence that the lack of trust results in a 'never-ending series of policy conflicts' with stakeholders constantly trying to undo the other's actions (Jongh and Captain 1999: 5).

There are several examples of how NPS cooperative programming strengthens existing networks through its ability to span across several jurisdictional lines. For example, the NPS provides technical expertise and computer capabilities in areas that small NGOs might not have (e.g., developing GIS databases of natural resources in a given area or creating maps for brochures). This might be an example of expertise spanning. In implementing these NPS programs, the NPS operates both horizontally and vertically across jurisdictional lines. The NPS relies on partnerships created through these programs to effectively achieve its mission when interests and jurisdictions overlap. One example is the Appalachian Trail, which runs through the lengths of the Great Smokey Mountains National Park and Shenandoah National Park. To protect the trail and conserve its surroundings for future hikers, the NPS must coordinate with the U.S. Forest Service, state parks and agencies, private landowners, and nonprofit organizations such as the Appalachian Trail Conservancy. The National Trails System Program allows the NPS to allocate funding for this partnership to protect its shared interests (NPS, 2014b: 14).

In other cases, the NPS may not have any landholdings in relation to its programming. Such is the case with National Heritage Areas Program (NHAs). Heritage Areas preserve 'natural, cultural, historic, and scenic resources ... considered uniquely representative of the American experience' (National Park System Advisory Board 2006, 3). The NPS is materially involved in supporting the creation and management of these areas by providing technical and financial assistance.

NPS matching grants are also an important tool that the NPS has. These grants allow NGOs or local governments to leverage what might otherwise be insufficient funding to achieve a particular goal (e.g., put in a public access point, print brochures).

Finally, programming and collaboration is a lower cost model of operating and in some areas, a more politically feasible alternative to federal landholdings. State and local governments and NGOs may be able to further the NPS's mission of protecting natural and cultural resources of national significance without the NPS actually owning the land itself.

These collaborative benefits are intermediate outcomes and are inputs in the production of the final programmatic outputs. Thus it is important to recognize value added in between the initial input (financial and technical assistance) and the final value of programmatic outputs to arrive at an accurate estimate of cooperative programs.

Calculating the value of cooperative programs

Calculating the value of cooperative programs is far more challenging than for parks. We propose three different methods to estimate the value of cooperative programs. Method #1 is based on Chapter 2's TEV model. Method #2 is a finer-scale method more tailored to small individual programs or projects in which the NPS is just one of many contributors to the program or project. The first method is appropriate if NPS resources or funding is responsible for the entire value created. The second method is most appropriate when the NPS is just one of many contributors to the total value of the project. Of course, this same method can be used by any state, local agency, or NGO to also calculate its share of a joint project's benefits. Method #3 is when methods #1 and #2 are used in conjunction with one another. This method can be used in cases where the first method is the only way to approximate the total economic value of that output (e.g., a historic site or natural area being protected) but the local sponsor must also provide resources or funding to provide the public with the value of that output. Hence in this third case, there is a need to adjust the total value of the NPS program that the local sponsor helped to facilitate. Thus we call this hybrid approach Method #3.

Method #1: Adapting the TEV Function

In Chapter 2, the total economic value of each of the four broad categories of NPS programs was estimated using a willingness to pay (WTP) survey of the general public. The resulting WTP equation allows an analyst to calculate the per household value of an additional: (a) historic sites or buildings protected; (b) acres the NPS transfers to the community for recreation purposes; (c) a natural area of importance to a local community that NPS helped to protect; and (d) the number of schoolchildren attending programs produced by the NPS (although in this case it may also be possible to use the methods shown in Chapter 5 on education).

Using Method #1, the analyst would use the results from Chapter 2's WTP equation for the TEV *per household* of one more unit of output. For example, if NPS is solely responsible for transferring 10 acres of Federal land to a community to provide recreational open space, that value could be calculated from Table 2.7 as 10 times $15.20 per acre, or $152 per household.

The total value of the transfer would be calculated by multiplying the $152 by the number of households living in the area that would benefit from this open space. This could be the number of households living nearby the open space that would walk their dogs, jog, or go bird watching there. For example, if there are a thousand households that live within walking or jogging distance, then the total value would be $152,000. The same process would apply to protection by the NPS of natural landmarks or historic buildings facilitated by the NPS. The dollar values per household could be obtained from Table 2.7 and multiplied by the number of households benefitting from protection. Of course, this estimate assumes that there is no additional cost necessary from the local sponsor for the household to realize the benefits of the open space, Natural Landmark, or Historic Site. That is, all the funding is from the NPS and the community would not have needed to spend any of its own money for the households to realize or enjoy the benefits of the resource provided by the NPS. If the community must match the grant or install facilities such as parking or signage, then the hybrid method (Method #3) discussed below is needed to adjust what might be thought of as the *gross* value from Table 2.7 to the *net* benefits to the community of the resource provided by the NPS program.

Method #2: Estimating the value of NPS grants and other contributions to small-scale projects

This method is most useful when the NPS is just one partner that provides the protection of the historic building or natural area or recreation site. For example, the NPS might have provided a cost-share grant that funded 50% of the acquisition or recreation site facilities needed to provide safe public access. Alternatively, the NPS may have provided technical expertise in design, mapping, or inventory. All these functions can be valued at the wage rate of the NPS employees or the alternative cost that the program partner would have had to pay a consulting firm to provide that service necessary for the final output to be completed. For example, let's say the NPS program facilitates public access to a site used for recreation (e.g., a boat ramp, design of wildlife observation structure, interpretive sign). If the NPS or the partner stakeholders can estimate the value of that final output in dollar terms, then the percentage of NPS contribution to the total project cost can be used to apportion the benefit of the final output to the NPS program that facilitated the project.

While we provide an actual example of this for a boat ramp at our case study site (Chesapeake Bay), it is easy to visualize how this analysis could be performed, but it can be challenging in practice. For example, take the case of a wildlife observation structure that an NPS employee designed for a partner agency or NGO. Assume the NGO will pay the full cost of constructing the structure. The analyst would need to know: (a) the total cost of the structure the NPS employee designed. This total cost would include site preparation, construction of the structure, and making any other investments needed to make the structure suitable for visitor use; and (b) estimating the time cost of the NPS employees that helped design the structure. This would require estimating the labor rates and hours of the NPS employees used in this design or the cost that a consulting firm would have charged for the design.

Dividing (b)/(a) yields the percentage of total cost the NPS share; and finally (c) is the economic value of the output of the overall project. Multiplying (b/a) by (c) yields the dollar value of the NPS contribution of that NPS program. While for the wildlife observation deck the users are recreation visitors, for other projects or programs users could be school-children attending an environmental or Historic Site educational field trip. To estimate this economic value would require an estimate of the number of visitors that would be or are using the wildlife viewing platform, and the value of per visitor of the wildlife viewing taking place. Many county and state agencies have mechanical visitor counters or can estimate use if they are willing to go to the site on representative days and count visitors. The value per day of wildlife viewing is available from U.S. Fish and Wildlife Service's National Survey of Fishing, Hunting and Wildlife Associated Recreation (https://wsfrprograms.fws.gov/subpages/nationalsurvey/nat_su rvey2016.pdf) or U.S. Geologic Survey's Benefit Transfer Toolkit (https:// my.usgs.gov/benefit-transfer/).

None of these data requirements are insurmountable but nonetheless would take some effort to obtain the data. The same thought process would be followed if the NPS employee performed the background research to design and develop an interpretative sign or brochure for a historic site or building. For example, if NPS design contributed 40% of the total cost of the project, then the NPS program that allowed the NPS to provide the design would be credited with 40% of the total value of the final output. Of course, this same procedure would work to calculate the economic benefits of the other agency or NGO partners in the same project. The key accuracy check is at the end of the allocation process the analyst should make sure the sum of total benefits anticipated by all partners does exceed the total benefits of the project itself.

The conceptual foundation of this method is based on the idea that the total value of any output can be partitioned to the value of the inputs used to produce that output. In economics this idea is called 'product exhaus-tion' (Young and Loomis, 2014: 58). While the idea applies to competitive firms or companies, we appeal to the logic of that method for NGOs or county and state agencies. These entities must compete against one another for 'competitive grants' from the NPS or for scarce NPS employee time for their project, i.e., scarce NPS labor. Competitive grants are a category of the Land and Water Conservation Fund (Vincent, 2018, of Congressional Research Service). Further, we must make an additional assumption that the project would not have been feasible if the NPS had not participated. That is, in absence of the 'below market' or even 'free' (from the collaborators' point of view, not society's) contribution of NPS labor or data products (e.g., GIS maps) that the project would have not been financially feasible and hence not built. Thus, the NPS is considered an essential input to producing a viable project. If these assumptions are not applicable to the particular project, then the estimate of the benefits calculated in Method #2 would be an overestimate.

Method #3: A hybrid approach of methods #1 and #2

In many cases the analyst must adopt a hybrid approach for two reasons: (a) it is necessary to use the TEVs from Table 2.7 to estimate the program or project value because it is difficult to obtain data or derive a project or program's specific value; and (b) the NPS program provides only a portion of the total cost and the sponsoring agencies and/or NGO stakeholders must also contribute money and land to bring the entire project to fruition. Method #3 involves taking the valuation approach from Method #1 but netting out the cost to the sponsor to perform any additional construction or added labor to the project or program value in order for the community to realize the full benefit provided by the NPS program. That is, the analyst needs to subtract from the total *gross* community value calculated from Table 2.7 in Chapter 2 the costs to the local sponsor to arrive at a *net* value to the community. Thus, in the example of Method #1, the total economic value of 10 acres of Federal lands transferred by the NPS to become open space is $152 per household. As before, if there are 1,000 households that would benefit, the total value is $152,000. However, assume for this example that the local sponsor must construct parking and trails. If the cost of parking and trails is $25,000, then the net total value of the open space, which is ready for the public to realize its benefits, is $152,000 minus the $25,000 or $127,000. Thus, $127,000 is the net value of the NPS program that made possible the transfer of the lands to the community.

Case study of Chesapeake Bay Office of the NPS

This next section uses the Chesapeake Bay Office (CHBA) as a case study to illustrate the many dimensions of the value of NPS programs. The Chesapeake Bay is located on the mid-Atlantic coast, surrounded by the states of Maryland and Virginia as well as the District of Columbia. The bay includes 17 million people that live within the watershed, which covers 64,000 square miles (Phillips and McGee, 2014). There are 11,684 miles of coastline on the bay, more than the entire west coast of the USA (Chesapeake Bay Program, 2016a).

The ecological resources of the Chesapeake Bay region are noteworthy for its diversity and abundance. Equally so, the region is also remarkably culturally and historically rich. It is home to some of the earliest sites of European settlers, Revolutionary War and Civil War battlefields, and indigenous American Indian heritages that continue to this day (NPS, 2014a: 3).

The watershed is characterized by numerous overlapping political juris-dictions, multiple uses (housing, industry, recreation, agriculture, fishing, transportation, etc.), and competing public and private interests. These characteristics make it a classic example of a 'commons' problem—one agent's actions affect everyone in the watershed. Since no single entity has control of the region, partnerships and coordination are required in order to ensure that the Chesapeake Bay will be healthy and sustaining in the future.

The NPS in the Chesapeake Bay watershed

The CHBA of the NPS is responsible for managing all of the NPS pro-grams, trails, and partnerships related to the Chesapeake Bay watershed. Studying the benefits of cooperative programming in this region offers the unique opportunity to understand how the NPS can create value through this large landscape using a collaborative network of partnerships. There is huge potential: one estimate places the marginal added ecosystem service values of a restored Chesapeake Bay at over $22 billion per year (Phillips and McGee, 2014: 23). While the NPS is just one small player of many in the region, the potential benefit to be gained by NPS participation are orders of magnitude larger than the annual NPS office budget (less than one-tenth of 1%).

To better understand the value that NPS cooperative programming pro-vides in the Chesapeake Bay, qualitative interviews with CHBA leadership (Doherty and Copping, 2015) were undertaken. These interviews revealed the CHBA to work:

- *Locally* with small partners, landowners, and schools to increase public access, build visibility, educate youth, and install interpretive signage throughout the Chesapeake Bay region. It provides financial and tech-nical assistance to local governments, small social sector groups, and schools in order to empower them to carry out its goals.
- *Regionally* with partners around the bay, contributing to trail planning and management. It works to connect disparate public access sites into a cohesive and thematic experience along the National Trails, creat-ing resources and guides for visitors, and collaborating on conservation efforts.
- *Watershed-wide* with the Chesapeake Bay Program partners to restore the water quality across the watershed, and with groups such as the Chesapeake Conservation Partnership to create strategies to increase public access and landscape conservation.

We organize the Chesapeake Bay Program case study around Choi and Marlowe's (2012: 28–30) four potential functions that NPS programs can provide. Specifically: (a) funding; (b) coordination and management; (c) technical expertise and financial assistance; (d) organizational leveraging.

Funding

In the Chesapeake Bay, the NPS provides partners with federal grants for a variety of uses. These grants can be given to social sector organizations, state or local government agencies, or educational institutions. Often these grants go to support the creation of waysides, brochures, or the public access sites themselves.

Not surprisingly, financial assistance was often the first thing mentioned by partners when asked about their relationship with the NPS. They can be fundamental to the financial feasibility of achieving the partner's goals. They are also used to leverage additional funding and grants, as shown in Figure 7.1, taken from the CHBA Strategy and Operation Plan. The NPS grant of $14.7 million is matched by an additional $18.4 million from partners to yield a total of $33.1 million. Thus, for every $1 of NPS money leverages an additional $1.26 for a total effect of $2.26. Applying the 2.26 to the NPS $14.7 yields the $33.1 in Figure 7.1.

Technical expertise and assistance

The NPS also provides assistance to partners in the form of designing interpretive resources or access points, training individuals, providing capacity-building workshops, or helping partners meet compliance standards. The President of the Potomac Conservancy noted this contribution in the assistance that CHBA brings to the Potomac River conservation efforts:

> [The] NPS can use their experience from other river segment planning, and we can also benefit from their technical expertise in things like their mapping capabilities.

> (Belin, 2016)

NPS Chesapeake Bay
Office = $14.7 million

Generated $33 million in
total awarded funds

Figure 7.1 CHBA financial assistance leverage ratio
Source: NPS (2014a: 29).

The CHBA does not account for staff time devoted to providing technical assistance to specific partners or projects. This makes defining the exact outcomes and contributions of the office in this area very difficult. If the NPS wishes to value its programs, it will be important that the NPS starts tracking staff time devoted by specific employees to providing NPS programming to stakeholders.

Coordination and management

In addition to working one-on-one with partners, the NPS and CHBA coordinate and manage groups of stakeholders. These groups can range from informal, ad hoc working groups to formal, federally mandated, institutions such as the Chesapeake Bay Watershed Plan implementation teams. The CHBA also coordinates trail planning and compliance for the water trails, which necessitates working with a variety of stakeholders.

The office also takes a leadership role in the Chesapeake Conservation Partnership, convening a group of over 50 different partners operating at all levels of the Chesapeake Region. The goal is to 'benefit multiple values, including economic sustainability; scenic, historic, and cultural heritage; working lands; important wildlife habitat; water quality and supply; and overall quality of life.' (Chesapeake Conservation Partnership | Our Partners, 2016) These efforts can be broadly categorized under the CHBA strategic goal to 'Partner, Collaborate, and Manage.'

The Director of Planning and Recreational Resources at the Virginia Department of Conservation and Recreation noted:

> [The] NPS is the hub for connecting partners throughout the bay by convening and coordinating meetings with different state and local agencies. They play a critical role and we know that we can count on their support.
>
> (Poole, 2016)

Partners identified specific ways that the CHBA provides value through its coordination and management. The most commonly mentioned being: (a) facilitating the exchange of information; (b) connecting the multiple attributes of a place (historical, cultural, environmental, recreational) that contribute its value; and (c) building trust and resolving conflict.

Additionally, coordinating and managing formal partnerships results in shared outputs that can be jointly used by all stakeholders in the future. The development of *LandScope Chesapeake*, a GIS database, and the Chesapeake Bay Watershed Public Access Plan are good examples (NPS, 2013).

Occasionally, NPS coordination produces increased funding for all partners. For example, the 'Rivers of the Chesapeake' proposal submitted by several collaborating partners received $11 Million from the 2016 Land and Water Conservation Fund (LWCF) allocations (Department of the Interior 2015). These grant funds were awarded to protect important watershed-wide access segments. The proposal was the result of years of work by the Chesapeake Conservation Partnership, with NPS convening partners and coordinating the proposal logistics, including weekly coordination calls (Doherty and Copping, 2015).

Organizational leveraging

The NPS provides partners with exposure and connections to a nationwide network of parks and programs. While this service often works in conjunction with its coordination and management function (as was likely the case with the 'Rivers of the Chesapeake' proposal), it is distinct in that the network of partners does not need to be formally coordinated by the agency to gain value from the relationship.

All interviewees mentioned the strength of the NPS brand, and how their organization has benefited by association: an example of the NPS leveraging its brand by producing brochures for various partners. To the public, this consistency creates the perception of a unified Chesapeake Bay experience.

Every partner mentioned this to some extent: '[The] NPS connects smaller organizations to a larger message and story' (Cerino, 2016). Stakeholder engagement and expansion is important, but particularly so in watersheds when effects of pollution are literally felt downstream. The most visible manifestation of this value is the 'Find Your Chesapeake' website (NPS and Chesapeake Conservancy, 2016).

The previous sections describe services the CHBA provides through its programming, presenting various benefits to the public and its partners. These are helpful to understand *how* its partners and the public benefit from CHBA operations.

Most analysis of NPS programming considers only the benefits transferred to partners through financial and technical assistance. These serve as inputs into each partners' own outputs. The qualitative analysis illustrates the wide variety in *what* the benefits of each service are, and are not limited to financial and technical assistance.

However, not all of the collaborative benefits identified by CHBA partners are easily defined and captured in economic valuations. The value of the CHBA is not just an aggregation of the tangible outputs of its programs. Cooperative programming may also generate value through collaborative process outcomes: intermediate process outcomes make the collaborative process more efficient and effective, ultimately magnifying the benefits of the program outputs of the NPS and its partners. In economic terms, *the collaborative outcomes lower transaction costs and make the network process more efficient in delivering benefits.*

Frameworks for assessing the value of the CHBA

This section discusses how knowledge about NHAs, network analysis, and systems-based models can be applied to increase our understanding of the contribution of the CHBA.

NHAs

The NHA model has generated considerable recent interest. A report by the National Park System Advisory Board recognized the 'new dimension' that NHAs bring to the agency, and recommended that the NPS adopt formal policies and performance measures, and conduct further research so that they might 'maximize the benefit' of the model (National Park System Advisory Board, 2006: 4, 24). The National Park Second Century Commission called on Congress to authorize and fund NHAs to 'advance the 21st-century National Park idea' (National Parks Conservation Association, 2009, 43).

CHBA programs and benefits (as described by partners in the qualitative interviews) are in almost perfect alignment with this theoretical model. Brenda Barrett, former National Coordinator of Heritage Areas for NPS and current Editor of the *Living Landscape Observer*, noted that instead of using 'National Heritage' the CHBA creates a shared sense of place around the idea of a Chesapeake Bay landscape. Its watertrails serve as the backbone and glue that provides a collaborative framework for coordinated action, and leverage its connections and the NPS brand to add value to the partnerships (Barrett, 2016).

Network analysis

The field of network analysis informs our understanding of how to assess areas of programmatic value. In his work, Agranoff focuses on defining the recipient(s) of these network benefits (rather than trying to define myriad potential benefits created) and creates four categories (2008, 329–332):

- Personal benefits
- Agency benefits
- Network process outcomes
- Tangible network outcomes.

Agranoff notes that all recipients of the network benefits are relevant, whether they are in the form of an individual, a single agency, or the network as a whole. He also distinguishes between network process outcomes, and tangible network outcomes. Process outcomes are related to 'bringing administrators and specialists together,' 'multi-agency problem solving', 'exchanging ideas and resources' in a common forum, and synergistically addressing cross-agency problems' (2008, 330–331). CHBA partners identified many of these same outcomes in interviews.

Agranoff defines tangible network outcomes as studies and datasets, financial resources, joint plans or policy, new agreements, and capacity building training and exercises that would not happen outside of the network. These tangible outcomes are more easily measured, and in the CHBA's case would include things like joint segment planning or 'Rivers of the Chesapeake' funding.

Systems-based model

The purpose of this section is to combine the insights gained from qualitative interviews with lessons learned from network analysis, collaborative management literature, and the considerable overlap between the CHBA and NHAs.

A systems-based model builds on the work of Levan et al. (2010) and shows the cyclic nature of how program inputs and collaborative strategies build upon each other to generate and improve upon program outputs.

Figure 7.2 uses this model in the CHBA context and includes an overlay of the programmatic services, as defined by Choi and Marlowe (2012), and network outcomes, as defined by Agranoff (2008). The dotted line represents how the intermediate outcomes feedback into the system, adding value to the final programmatic outputs.

The programmatic services of 'coordination and management' and 'organizational leveraging' create considerable value through these intermediate outcomes, and it is these outcomes that are not recognized by standard valuation techniques. In fact, NPS leaders who work in these collaborative environments all noted that they measure their progress and success by these process and governance outcomes (Parker, 2016; Doherty and Copping, 2015; Kish, 2016; Barrett, 2016). This is indicative of their value, and this systems-based model accounts for these effects.

CHBA Program Theory Model

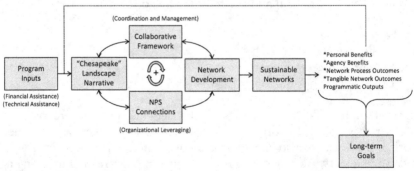

Figure 7.2 CHBA program theory model, with overlaid Agranoff and Choi and Marlowe definitions

Source: Author.

Quantitative analysis: economic valuations

The qualitative analysis section describes many of the various benefits that CHBA generates for the public and its partners. While many of these intermediate outputs and benefits could be quantified in one form or another (e.g., number of stakeholders attending a meeting, number of cooperative agreements signed, reduction in number of lawsuits), they are often not quantified. This lack of quantification may be due, in part, to lack of systematically collected data or inconsistent record keeping. This section illustrations valuation Method #2 for programmatic services: how to determine the contribution of the NPS to collaborative projects with partners. A full economic valuation of every CHBA output is not possible within the scope of this chapter. We hope that future research adapts and refines valuation efforts not only in Chesapeake Bay but the hundreds of other areas that NPS programs are involved in. To make these advances requires convincing NPS staff that if they wish to value their programs they must document their staff's contributions to collaborative programs and projects.

Details of Method #2 to attribute use values to NPS programs for a long-lived project

To find an agency's proportional contribution to a project, it is first necessary to calculate the total annual benefit that the project brings. To do so we will rely on use value, determined by multiplying the number of expected users times the per-user value of the project. In this example, the users are recreation visitors, but users could be school children attending an environmental or historic site educational field trip. We analyze the benefits of public access recreation sites, valued using an original survey of users, an analysis of users travel behavior, or the benefit transfer method, which relies on values in the literature (see Rosenberger and Loomis, 2017 for more details on this method). However, to some extent, all other valuations could follow the same general model, though would be somewhat more abstract.

To find the annual value of a public access site, we take the value per unit of use (Use_{value} in \$s) and multiply that by the number of users (per year):

$$\text{Benefit}_{Annual} = \text{Use}_{value} * \text{Users}$$

In many projects, it is the long-term value of the site that is of interest. By long term value we mean the number of years the project is expected to be functional. We insert this recurring annual benefit into the present value (PV) formula:

$$PV \text{ of Benefit}_{Total} = \sum_{t=1}^{N} \left(\text{Use}_{Value} * \text{Users}_t \right) * \left(1 + r \right)^{-t}$$

Where $\sum$ is the summation sign indicating we are summing the benefits occurring each of t years over N, which is the total number of years the project will be in operation. r is the interest rate or what is called the discount rate since constant dollar future benefits are discounted back to the present, hence the name present value. Note the future benefits may be increasing due to expected increases in visitation[2], but these total dollar values are discounted back to account for the delayed timing of these benefits relative to today. This formula gives us the total value that the public access site gives over its lifetime of T years. As most readers know, spreadsheets have formulas to automate the actual calculation of PV.

To calculate net PV (NPV) we must subtract the PV of the costs from the present value of the benefits. The PV of the costs of the project or program ($Cost_{Total}$) usually contains two elements: (a) the initial costs—often acquisition or construction costs (which is essentially in PV terms to start with) and (b) the PV of any recurring maintenance costs, management costs, and other operating costs over the lifetime of the project (T years). The same formula for PV is adapted to calculate the present value of the costs.

To calculate the NPS contribution percentage, one would add together all the relevant items that the NPS provided divided by the $Cost_{Total}$. In this example, the NPS contribution would include financial assistance provided through grants (*FinAsst*, measured in dollars). If the NPS provided technical assistance, we would use the cost of hours spent on the project (*TechAsst*, measured in hours). We can inquire about how many hours different NPS employees worked on this project (*TechAsst*) and their respective wage rate to calculate the mean wage (*MeanWage*, measured in $/hour):

$$NPS\% \text{ Contribution} = \frac{FinAsst + (TechAsst * MeanWage)}{Cost_{Total}}$$

We can then multiply this percentage by the total *net* present value of a project (PV of the benefits minus the PV of the cost):

$$= NPS\% \text{ Contribution}(\%) * \sum_{T=1}^{N}\left(\left(Use_{Value} * Users_t - Cost_{Total}\right) * (1+r)^{-t}\right)$$

This gives us an estimate of the total value that the NPS creates through their collaboration on the project. The advantage of this method is that we do not need to worry about double counting because partners can use the same formula to determine its own percentage of contribution. As long as the sum of all the partners' contributions does not exceed 100% there is no double counting.

Applied empirical example

Using data from CHBA operations gives an opportunity to illustrate this method with a real-world example. We apply the formula discussed above to a recently developed public access site in the Chesapeake Bay watershed: the Fort Monroe Kayak Launch.

Table 7.2 NPV estimates for Fort Monroe Kayak Launch (25-year lifespan) and the estimated value created by NPS proportional to its contributions

	Per use visitor value ($)	NPV	Total NPS value
Low-bound estimate	$34	$429,706	$154,694
High-bound estimate	$76	$1,141,042	$410,775

Since the NPS does not actually own or manage the kayak launch, the NPS only has access to usage data that its partners collect. We were able to collect enough data from the kayak site at Fort Monroe to make a partial estimate of public value. It is important to emphasize that this estimate is very conservative because we used only confirmed usage data from the kids' programming over 11 weeks (which amounted to 990 kids) during the summer. We did not add any general public visitors, which would increase its value.

Table 7.2 shows the results of this analysis. The NPV of the kayak launch site is based on various estimates of per visitor value. We use benefits transfer estimates generated by the recreation use values database compiled by Dr. Rosenberger at Oregon State University (http://recvaluation.forestry.oregonstate.edu/), as well the travel cost demand method estimate by (Neher, Duffield, and Patterson (2013). We recognize the valuation estimates are those of adults or families with children, and not solely children. However, rarely are estimates of benefits to just children available in the literature.

In order to calculate the present value, we used a discount rate of 3.125%, which is the recommended rate for federal water projects (USDA 2016b). Finally, we also assumed a 25-year lifespan for the launch site, with $5,000 of maintenance costs every 5 years.

To find the proportional contribution of NPS, we first found the financial assistance provided by NPS ($48,532). Then we made a conservative estimate of the hours of assistance provided and multiplied by the hourly cost (wages and benefits) per CHBA full-time equivalent employee. We used the full-time equivalent since CHBA does not track specific employees performing technical assistance. This calculation produces the technical assistance estimate. We estimated the total cost by adding the capital outlays to the staff time cost for NPS and its partners. The total NPS contribution is therefore:

$$\frac{FinAsst + (TechAsst * MeanWage)}{Cost_{Total}} = \frac{\$48,532 + (20hrs * \$54.69 / hr)}{\$137,244} = 36\%$$

Multiplying this NPS percentage of contribution by the NPV of the project gives the proportion of NPV that NPS contributed to the Fort Monroe Kayak Launch, over the projects 25-year lifespan.

The NPV in Table 7.2 represents the value of the kayak launch site (using only the 990 kids per summer). This estimate is likely a conservative lower bound because there is likely substantial visitor use of the kayak launch area by the general public which would increase the valuation substantially. Since many agencies have simple ways to count visitor use (e.g., parking lot counts or pneumatic hoses to measure vehicle traffic counts) it would not be very expensive for the agencies to develop more accurate estimates of use if they wished a more accurate estimate of the benefits.

Conclusions

At its most effective, the NPS leverages its partnerships, network, and organizational strengths to increase the scope and magnitude of its reach. In this manner, the NPS has the capacity to connect with the public in ways that other federal and state agencies cannot:

> The National Park Service is the public face of the federal Chesapeake Bay Program. Federally mandated regulation has very negative connotations with a lot of people. But with NPS involvement, it changes to a story about pride of place, heritage, education, and citizen stewardship. Danette Poole, Virginia DCR.
>
> (Poole, 2016)

The value of the cooperative programming that makes this transformation possible is not always easily quantified, but it has a substantial but often overlooked value. It is important to understand how programming and collaboration contribute to the full value of the NPS mission. This is the intent of former NPS Director Jarvis in his *Call to Action*: developing an awareness of the value cooperative programming that helps to connect the public to what the National Park Service does outside of parks themselves.

The spirit of this chapter is that it is the first of many economic analyses focused on NPS programming. To conduct such an analysis, a mixed-methods approach of qualitative and quantitative analysis is often necessary.

We believe that this chapter makes the following case:

1   **Cooperative programming generates value through collaborative process outcomes.** These outcomes make the collaborative process more efficient and effective, ultimately magnifying the program outputs of NPS and its partners.
2   When quantifiable, **it is possible to develop and employ methods to calculate a share of the public value** created from these program outputs to specific organizations within a collaborative partnership. This allows

for the creation of TEV whether using general household valuations in Table 2.7 in Chapter 2 or individual project-specific valuations.

The significance of this chapter lies largely in the qualitative analysis of collaborative process outcomes and their role in value creation. When we started researching this topic, a popular description of the value of the NPS cooperative programming was as the 'glue' between disparate partners in the region. The qualitative analysis has put this vague description of value into context. The primary source data reveal how the NPS leverages its connections within a collaborative framework and develops a shared sense of heritage and place. These factors contribute to a strong network of partners, which results in human capital, infrastructure, financial, and external process benefits. These outcomes make working to conserve and restore the Chesapeake Bay more efficient.

Former Director Jarvis calls collaborating with partners the 'future of the Park Service' (Jarvis, 2015) because it allows the agency to do more with less funding. Programming also allows the NPS to collaborate with partners outside of its landholdings. This enables the NPS to 'scale up' its conservation efforts with the potential to create public value (ecological, cultural, historical, recreational, and economic) on a large landscape level that extends past park borders (NPS, 2014b, 3).

As the NPS makes plans to scale up its mission for the next 100 years, it needs to look no further than its role as organizational 'glue'. Its cooperative programming has the ability to span levels of governments, geographical boundaries, interest groups, and ideologies in order to effectively connect the American public to its natural and cultural history. There is real public value in performing that role well.

Notes

1 https://www.nps.gov/subjects/nationalregister/database-research.htm.
2 In some circumstances it may be possible to forecast future visitation over time based on demographics such as expected population growth in an area that would reflect this change in users over time and incorporate it into the model.

References

Agranoff, R. 2008. Enhancing performance through public sector networks: mobilizing human capital in communities of practice. *Public Performance & Management Review* 31(3): 320–347.

Barrett, Brenda. 2016. Personal interview with Brenda Barrett.

Belin, Hedrick. 2016. Personal interview with Hedrick Belin.

Cerino, Chris. 2016. Personal interview with Chris Cerino.

Choi, F. and T. Marlowe. 2012. The Value of America's Greatest Idea: Framework for Total Economic Valuation of National Park Service Operations and Assets and Joshua Tree National Park Total Economic Value Case Study. A report provided to the NPS, Harvard Kennedy School of Government. https://www.nps.gov/resources/upload/Task-4-Joshua-Tree-Case-Study-The-Value-of-America-s-Greatest-Idea-Choi-and-Marlowe-2012.pdf.

Department of the Interior. 2015. National Park Service Fiscal Year 2016 Budget Justifications. Department of the Interior: NPS. http://www.nps.gov/aboutus/budget.htm.

Doherty, J. and S. Copping. 2015. Personal interview with NPS Chesapeake Bay Office leadership.

Jarvis, J. 2015. Conversation with NPS Director Jon Jarvis.

Jongh, P. E. de and S. Captain. 1999. *Our Common Journey: A Pioneering Approach to Cooperative Environmental Management.* London, UK ; New York, USA: Zed Books.

Kish, M. 2016. Personal interview with Meghan Kish, Superintendent of Blackstone River Valley National Heritage Corridor.

Laven, D., C. Ventriss, R. Manning, and N. Mitchell. 2010. Evaluating U.S. National Heritage Areas: theory, methods, and application. *Environmental Management* 46(2): 195–212.

National Park Service. 2013a. Chesapeake Bay Watershed Public Access Plan. Annapolis, MD: National Park Service. http://executiveorder.chesapeakebay.net/Public_Access_Plan_FINAL.pdf.

National Park Service. 2013b. National Park Service Programs. Washington DC: Office of Policy.

NPS. 2014a. National Park Service Chesapeake Bay Office: 2014 Strategy and Operational Review. Business Management Group.

NPS. 2014b. Scaling Up: Collaborative Approaches to Large Landscape Conservation. NPS. http://www.largelandscapenetwork.org/wp-content/uploads/2014/10/2014NPS_ScalingUp.pdf.

National Park System Advisory Board. 2006. Charting a Future for National Heritage Areas. https://www.nps.gov/orgs/1412/upload/Charting-a-Future-NHAreport.pdf.

National Parks Conservation Association. 2009. Advancing the National Park Idea: Second Century Commission Report. https://www.google.com/url?sa=t&rct=j&q=&esrc=s&source=web&cd=1&ved=0ahUKEwiMoKnF35rKAhUIwj4KHcjND08QFggdMAA&url=http%3A%2F%2Fwww.nps.gov%2Fcivic%2Fresources%2FCommission_Report.pdf&usg=AFQjCNGItw-GdrBllNGAUCoTIPIFdmiwzQ&sig2=enJjQmEoAQ-zjFwYkLIQcw.

Neher, C., J. Duffield, and D. Patterson. 2013. Valuation of national park system visitation: the efficient use of count data models, meta-analysis, and secondary visitor survey data. *Environmental Management* 52(3): 683–698.

Parker, G. 2016. Personal interview with Superintendent Giles Parker of Boston Harbor Islands National Recreation Area.

Phillips, S. and B. McGee. 2014. The Economic Benefits of Cleaning up the Chesapeake: Valuation of the Natural Benefits Gained by Implementing the Chesapeake Clean Water Blueprint. Key-Log Economics, LLC and Chesapeake Bay Foundation.

Poole, D. 2016. Personal interview with Danette Poole.

Rosenberger, R. and J. Loomis. 2017. Benefit Transfer. In P. Champ, K. Boyle and T. Brown (Eds.). *A Primer on Nonmarket Valuation.* 2nd Edition. Dordrecht, The Netherlands: Springer.

Schneider, M., J. Scholz, M. Lubell, D. Mindruta, and M. Edwardsen. 2003. Building consensual institutions: networks and the National Estuary Program. *American Journal of Political Science* 47(1): 143–158.

The Urban Agenda—Urban Parks and Programs (US National Park Service). n.d. Retrieved 1 February 2016 from http://www.nps.gov/subjects/urban/Urban-Agenda.htm.

Young, R. and J. Loomis. 2014. *Determining the Economic Value of Water: Concepts and Methods*, 2nd Edition. New York, NY: RFF Press.

8 Sustainable funding for the National Park Service

Linda J. Bilmes and Jonathan B. Jarvis

The preceding chapters identify a number of ways in which the National Park System enriches society. We find that the American public places a value on the National Park lands and programs that exceeds $90 billion— at least 30 times higher than the annual budget it receives from Congress. We also show that the existence of the National Park Service (NPS) creates value in areas as diverse as carbon sequestration and intellectual property.

However, the funding the NPS receives from a combination of appropriations, visitors' fees, concessions, and philanthropy is inadequate to maintain and invest in this precious and valuable set of assets. Consequently, the agency is fighting an uphill battle to keep National Park Service units (NPS units) pristine and unspoiled as visitor numbers climb and climate change puts stress on the natural resources in many NPS units. The NPS has a $12 billion backlog of overdue maintenance projects, which includes roads, bridges, campgrounds, trails, and utilities, along with preventing forest fires and repairing historical monuments and visitor facilities.

Moreover, NPS has been forced to shut down more than 22 times since 1974, as a result of congressional budget disputes that have nothing to do with the agency itself. Unfortunately, the public's affection for the agency has made it easy to use as leverage in spending battles. This situation compounds the uncertainty over annual funding.

This chapter outlines the structure of NPS funding today and argues that it is inconsistent with the mission of the agency. We introduce a series of ideas that could alleviate financial pressures on the NPS in the short term and make its funding more sustainable over the next century.

Shortcomings of the current funding model

The NPS is currently funded through a complex formula that includes Federal discretionary budget appropriations, revenue generated from fees and concessions, private philanthropy, and in-kind donations. This model has failed to provide the agency with a stable, long-term source of funding. To fulfill its dual mission of providing public recreational opportunity as well as conservation in perpetuity, the agency needs a different, and more sustainable, funding structure.

The primary source of NPS funding is annual Federal appropriations. As shown in Figure 8.1 this budget has been relatively flat for more than two decades, resulting in an increased strain on the agency. In real terms, Federal outlays to NPS in 2018 were about $2.5 billion compared with $2.15 billion in 1999.

During this period, NPS received additional supplemental appropriations during some years, (e.g., in Fiscal Year (FY) 2009 for the American Recovery and Reinvestment Act (ARRA) and in 2013 and 2018 for hurricane recovery). Including these extra injections of funding, the 2018 budget was 8% less in real terms than 2009 (see Figure 8.2).

While funding has been flat, the number of visitors to NPS units has grown dramatically. In 1980, there were 198 million visitors. By 2015 the number of visitors had grown to 307 million (US Department of Interior, 2017). During the past decade, visitation rose 16%, from 285.6 million in 2009 to 330.1 million in 2017 (see Table 8.1). Congress has also designated 26 new NPS sites in the past decade, including the Stonewall National Monument in New York in 2016 and the World War I Memorial in Washington DC in 2014 (Comway, 2018)[1].

The agency also faces growing operational and maintenance responsibilities due to exogenous factors, such as increased population density adjacent to some NPS units and climate changes that are causing fires to burn longer and hotter, sea levels to rise, storm surges to be more damaging and wildlife patterns to change.

There are two main consequences of this mismatch between the NPS core workload and NPS core budget revenue. First, park superintendents have

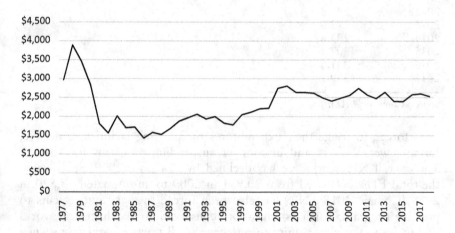

Figure 8.1 NPS appropriations FY1977–FY2018
Source: White House Budget Authority.

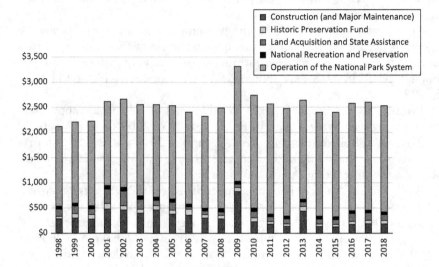

Figure 8.2 NPS real discretionary appropriations by account (including ARRA) FY1998–2018

Source: White House Budget Authority (2019).

Table 8.1 NPS visitation 2009–2017

Year	Number of visitors
2009	285.6
2010	281.3
2011	278.9
2012	282.8
2013	273.6
2014	292.8
2015	307.2
2016	331.0
2017	330.1

Source: Comway (2018).

been forced to triage their expenditures by allowing facilities to decline, hiring fewer workers and limiting or suspending programs for visitors. The overall NPS workforce has declined by 7% since 2009. Specifically, the total FTEs decreased from 20,991 in 2009 to an estimated 19,520 in 2018 (Comay, 2018). NPS has also been forced to make budget cuts to popular programs (such as education, conservation, and historical work) and to forgo the opportunity to purchase small tracts of privately owned land located inside NPS units even when they come up for sale at favorable prices.

The second consequence is that the agency has been forced to delay urgent maintenance and repairs. Decades of chronic underfunding for construction and maintenance have produced a maintenance backlog of nearly $12 billion across the NPS system. This means that some of the NPS core assets are deteriorating much faster than they can be replenished. Outlays for this category of the budget have dropped from an average of $312 million per year during the 1990s to an average of $286 million since 2000 (apart from the ARRA funding in 2009). The decline in the past 20 years is shown in Figure 8.3. The NPS unfunded maintenance backlog includes roads, waterways, visitor centers, trails, bridges and other infrastructure.

NPS funding structure

NPS appropriations

The NPS's appropriations are primarily in five accounts: basic park operations; construction and repair of infrastructure; assistance to state, local, tribal, and private land managers (National Recreation and Preservation account); grants to states and localities for historic preservation (Historic Preservation Fund); and land acquisition by both the NPS and the states (Land Acquisition and State Assistance account). None of these funds are suitable to ensure long-term viability.

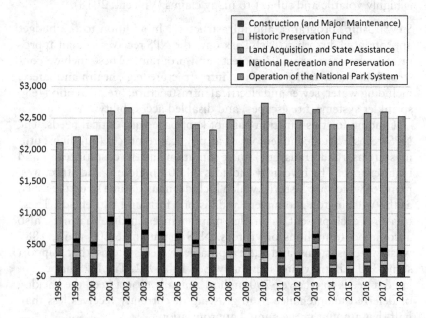

Figure 8.3 NPS real discretionary appropriations by account (excluding ARRA) FY1998–FY2018

Source: White House Budget Authority.

1   Direct park operations: The largest category of government funding is direct park operations, which fund salaries and routine maintenance. Congress appropriates a specific line-item amount to each of the 419 individual Park units. These totals are fixed in the budget process and cannot be changed by the Secretary or the Director without going back to Congress with a reprogramming request. Within each Park, the individual superintendents have limited flexibility on how to allocate the budget because the vast majority of expenditures are fixed costs (such as payroll and utilities).

2   The Land and Water Conservation Fund (LWCF): This is the principal source of funding used by four Federal land management agencies— the NPS, the Bureau of Land Management, the Forest Service, and the Fish and Wildlife Service. In addition, the LWCF provides grants to states for outdoor recreation purposes, which are administered through the NPS. Congress is authorized to draw up to $900 million annually through the LWCF (which derives the majority of its revenues from oil and gas leases on the Outer Continental Shelf) to purchase lands for outdoor recreation and conservation, but the money is not actually spent unless it is appropriated by Congress. The actual amount of appropriations has only exceeded the $400 million level in 14 years since the LWCF was established in 1965. The NPS receives or administers some 60% of the annual amount; however, the stream of funding is highly volatile and subject to many claims (Vincent, 2018).

3   Stewardship, programs, and infrastructure: In addition to the budget appropriated directly to each Park unit, the NPS receives a small appropriation for 'service-wide' projects and programs. These include construction, maintenance of critical infrastructure (e.g., health and safety, including water, sewer and electrical infrastructure, fire prevention (e.g. sprinkler systems, fire escapes) and disabled accessibility.

Funding for this function has not kept pace with critical needs. The NPS keeps a detailed inventory of its physical resources (buildings, utility systems, road, trails, etc.), their condition and the cost for repair and maintenance. The inventory includes 24,000 buildings and structures, many of which are historic, which include many unique structures such as the Washington Monument and historic forts and battlefields. These treasures each present a complex maintenance schedule that must also accommodate millions of visitors. NPS maintains 6,200 trails, 1887 wastewater systems and 1,529 potable water systems that support some 300 million visitors annually. See Table 8.2. The NPS has calculated it needs to receive $700 million annually to just keep the backlog of deferred maintenance from growing. It currently receives less than half that amount in the annual appropriation.

4   Other appropriated funds. NPS receives a small amount of funding through various other funds, including the Historic Preservation Fund

Table 8.2 NPS maintenance and repair backlog of capital needs as of September 30 2017

NPS asset inventory summary

Asset category	Number of asset locations	Facility condition index	Critical systems deferred maintenance	Deferred maintenance	Current replacement value	Quantity	Unit of measure
Buildings	24,879	0.090	$680,836,286	$2,059,805,808	$22,777,514,643	47,095,383	SqFt
Housing	3,870	0.107	$68,759,391	$181,619,412	$1,690,237,051	6,376,804	SqFt
Campgrounds	1,388	0.105	$16,428,505	$75,771,964	$723,503,131	12,668	Acres
Trails	6,260	0.095	$222,521,243	$462,205,902	$4,860,375,991	99,499,321	Lineal Ft
Waste water systems	1,887	0.133	$159,431,258	$270,602,289	$2,036,481,323	18,415,339	Gals/day
Water systems	1,529	0.110	$248,142,046	$420,456,287	$3,813,853,022	43,020,609	Gals/day
Unpaved roads	5,534	0.067	$74,137,380	$209,115,006	$3,118,914,261	N/A	N/A
Paved roads	11,978	0.219	N/A	$5,900,394,123	$26,940,518,097	N/A	N/A
All others	18,557	0.022	$1,114,081,046	$2,026,809,602	$90,255,127,651	N/A	N/A
TOTAL	75,882	0.074	$2,584,337,154	$11,606,780,393	$156,216,525,170	N/A	N/A

(supporting cultural and historic heritage projects outside of the actual National Parks, such as funding for places to be listed on the National Register of Historic Places), the National Recreation and Preservation Fund (assisting local governments and volunteer organizations) and the Centennial fund (offering matching funds for partner donations).

5   Transportation funds: The NPS also derives revenues from the Federal Highway Trust Fund (FHTF)[2] to help repair and maintain its 5553 miles of paved roads within national parks. Again, this source of funding is not sustainable. In 2016, the maintenance backlog of roads within the NPS was nearly $6 billion and it received only $268 million from the FHTF. Moreover, since 2008 the FHTF itself has required large transfers of general revenue to stay afloat. The Congressional Budget Office projects that outlays from the FHTF will exceed trust fund reserves by 2028, even if expiring trust fund taxes are extended (Congressional Budget Office, 2018).

In short, Federal funding provided to the NPS comes from a volatile mixture of revenue sources. These revenues have not kept pace with the growth in visitors or requirements for operating NPS, much less for the long-term sustainability of the system.

The level of federal funding is unlikely to change. As mandatory Federal expenditures (including entitlements and debt service) have grown to nearly 2/3 of the budget, there is growing pressure on the discretionary portion of the federal budget that supports NPS and other parts of the U.S. Department of Interior (DOI). Other land management agencies, including the Fish and Wildlife Service, the Bureau of Land Management, the Bureau of Indian Affairs, and the U.S. Geological Survey, are also facing funding shortfalls as a result of competition for the shrinking discretionary pie.

Non-government funding

Unlike the majority of Federal government entities, the NPS earns a significant share of its total budget through private concessions, user fees, partnerships, and philanthropy. Each Park has its own constellation of partners and sources of funding, so the same function may be funded differently from one unit to another. Some NPS units are able to support a wider range of visitor services than others, due to their specific funding circumstances. The task of managing these budgets is far greater than for a typical government program. Park superintendents may struggle to identify funding sources to support vital programs and amenities in their respective Park units.

The NPS is unique in terms of how it collects income from fees (including entrance fees, sporting, and other fees) and concessions (from hotels, tour operators, restaurants, shops within the NPS units). Currently, private companies receive concessions to manage visitor services in National Parks and to collect some visitor access fees.

Fees

Fees have been collected for 100 years to supplement federal appropriations. Currently, only 117 of the 418 NPS units charge entrance fees. Some NPS units do not collect entrance fees due to multiple entrances, the intermingling of Park boundaries with other private or state lands, or visitation being too low to justify the expense of collection. At the NPS units that do charge fees, these fees have remained low as part of a deliberate effort to make the NPS units available to all. For example, in 1916, when the NPS was established by Congress, the fee for automobile entry to Yellowstone was $10[3]. If inflation was applied to that fee, the entrance fee today would be $230 rather than the current $30.

The NPS also collects fees for activities such as camping, backcountry and river boating trips (e.g., the Colorado River through the Grand Canyon NP). Along with other Federal land agencies, NPS sells special passes (authorized by Congress) such as the annual America the Beautiful Pass ($80), the Lifetime Senior Pass ($80), and in some cases, annual passes for individual NPS units. The NPS waives fees for active duty military, fourth graders, and those with disabilities, and offers a few 'free' days per year to celebrate certain holidays.

In addition to entrance and camping fees, the NPS charges fees for commercial activities (e.g., filming of a TV commercial and hosting special events). These are charged on the basis of recovering some of the direct costs, (such as the cost of having a ranger to redirect traffic in the vicinity) with small additional levies based on the number of people involved. This rudimentary cost recovery does not include any overhead costs and does not attempt to earn a return from the use of the Park premises. For example, *Star Wars*, which grossed $5 billion, filmed a number of scenes in Death Valley National Park. The studio paid only the standard permit fees.

Fees contribute only a small fraction of the NPS overall budget. For example, in 2016, the NPS collected some $230 million in fee revenue, of which 15–18% was spent on the collection effort itself (paying for staff at Park entrances, handling, and auditing of the collection program). The fees are deposited into a U.S. Treasury Account and remain there until expended by the NPS. (The U.S. Treasury earns the interest on these accounts.) Each NPS unit that collects fees is allowed to retain 80% of those fees to be spent within that Park. The remaining 20% is pooled and allocated competitively to those NPS units that do not collect any fees.

Due to geographic location and many other factors, there is a very wide variation among the NPS units in terms of visitation. The most-visited NPS units (which include the Great Smokies, Zion, Grand Canyon, Yosemite, Yellowstone, Acadia, and other iconic places) generate the vast majority of fee income while units that are more remote (e.g., Gates of the Arctic National Park in Alaska and North Cascades in Washington) produce almost none. The 80/20 rule means that the NPS Director has only a limited amount of leeway to redistribute fee revenues among the NPS units, even though our study of passive use benefit shows that the U.S. public places a high value on conserving Park units even if they do not visit.

Moreover, there are restrictions in how fee income can be spent. It may be used to pay for expenses related to the visitor experience (such as visitor information, signage, enhancement to visitor facilities and attractions, trail improvements) but not for day-to-day basic Park operations. This policy is supported by the NPS leadership, which believes that limits on the use of fee income are necessary to prevent Congress from trying to lower its NPS annual appropriations for operations.

Concessions

The NPS administers more than 575 concession contracts that, in total, gross over $1 billion annually. These concessioners employ more than 25,000 people in a variety of fields during peak seasons, providing services ranging from food service and lodging to whitewater rafting adventures and motor coach tours.

The concessions include private hotels, guides and outfitters, food services, and souvenir sales, some of which have been a part of the National Parks for over a century. Most of the original facilities have been purchased and restored by the NPS, often using local materials and local architectural styles[4]. However, the NPS has not had sufficient funding to upgrade old (and historic) visitor accommodations to the level expected by modern visitors. (For example, many historic hotels still feature tiny rooms and shared bathrooms.)

Concessioners pay a franchise fee to the federal government based on the value of the contract. This franchise fee averages 5% on all contracts. However, a small fraction of contracts account for most of the income. Some 60 contracts generate 85% of total gross receipts, while three-quarters of contracts are under $500,000. The NPS collects approximately $80 million in franchise fees per year.

Like entrance fees, this funding is retained in the U.S. Treasury and there are restrictions on how the money can be used. The priority for the funding is to improve the quality of visitor facilities. The fund is often used to repair existing hotels and concession facilities or to pay down old existing possessory interest from past contracts.

The legal arrangements for managing these concessions in place from 1965 to 1996 gave the private companies operating the facilities a preferential right to renew their contracts if they performed satisfactorily. In addition, each time a company reinvested in the physical infrastructure, they accrued 'possessory interest' in that improvement. Over time and with multiple renewals of their contracts, the possessory interest grew to exceed the actual replacement value of the buildings. This created an absurd situation, in which the NPS or a new concession was obligated to pay the previous concession operator for the premises. For example, the main hotel concessioner at Grand Canyon accrued a higher amount each month than it paid out in the monthly franchise fee paid to the NPS. In other words, a private company was operating inside a National Park with nearly 100% occupancy, using government-owned buildings and each month the NPS owed them more money than they paid.

Congress revised the concessions law in 1996 to introduce more competition in the process, which has enabled the NPS to earn a better return on franchise fees. However, the new system has so far failed to entice many new entrants and has caused additional legal and management headaches to manage what is only a modest contribution to the NPS coffers.

Partnerships and philanthropy

In 1916, the idea that a private person would willingly donate land or money to the federal government was greeted with a great deal of political skepticism. Fortunately, the first director of the NPS, Stephen Mather, established a tradition of Park philanthropy. Early donors to NPS units included John D. Rockefeller, who donated the land and funding for Acadia National Park and Grand Teton National Park. This tradition of donating lands and funds has continued and grown ever since.

In 1967, Congress created the National Park Foundation (NPF) as a philanthropic partner of the NPS, charged with raising private funds to support the work of the Service. Since its inception, it has raised over $1 billion in private support for the NPS. However, there have always been concerns about the role of private philanthropy funding, and concern that it supplements the basic congressional support for the NPS units.

David Rockefeller, Jr., who served as the NPF Board chair, described a 'bright line' between the responsibilities of the Federal funding and that of philanthropy. His standard is that philanthropy should provide that margin of excellence over what can be done with Federal funds. However, the role of philanthropy has never been fully defined or institutionalized within NPS and continues to be somewhat ad hoc and continuously debated.

In the run-up to the 2016 NPS Centennial, the NPF worked in partnership with the NPS to mount a successful capital campaign ('Find Your Park'). The goal was to draw public attention not only to the NPS units themselves but to the concept of private philanthropy in the NPS units (including the National Park and 'Park specific' partners such as the Yosemite Conservancy). In total the campaign raised $400 million, which was returned to the NPS in the form of competitive grants for projects such as trail improvements, youth programs, interpretive exhibits, and infrastructure improvements. One of the major successes of this effort was the donation of 87,000 acres of private lands in Maine by Burt's Bees founder Roxanne Quimby accompanied by a $20 million endowment.

Many individual NPS units have philanthropic partners, often referred to as 'friends groups', (as well as partners who help with programming, volunteers, historical work, environmental stewardship, and many other aspects of Park engagement). The friends groups are authorized to solicit and accept funds (and at times lands or equipment) for the benefit of a specific Park. There are 214 friends groups in the NPS, contributing annually $349 million in direct grants or in-kind services to the NPS.

There is no question that philanthropy plays an important role in supporting NPS. Recognizing this role, Congress has enacted 'Challenge Cost Share' and 'Centennial Challenge' funds available to be used as a 1:1 match for major projects. However, while these kinds of partnership projects are high value, there are a multitude of regulatory impediments to their efficiency. For instance, the Federal funds and the donated funds cannot be intermingled into a single contract unless the private dollars are transferred to the government, a step often resisted by the donor. As a consequence, projects have to be segmented into 'who pays for what'.

More broadly, there are limits to what philanthropy can do. Raising money is time-consuming and costly for NPF and local friends groups. Moreover, money may be donated for purposes that are of greater importance to the donor than to the Park unit. It is far easier to raise funds for a new, highly visible project (e.g., building a new visitor center) than for the unglamorous maintenance and repair tasks that constitute the majority of the NPS capital backlog.

A further issue is that the amount of funds raised is unpredictable; varying from year to year, project to project and from one Park to another. The success of a particular campaign may depend on the energy and leadership at the local level and on overall economic conditions and fiscal policy. Finally, even the most successful friends groups contribute only a small amount to the overall. Of the 214 local friends groups, only fourteen produce revenue in excess of $6 million per year (Potrero Group, 2016) while the majority raise less than $1 million per year.

In summary, the current funding structure of the NPS is not aligned with the needs of the agency to achieve its perpetuity mission. Ideally, the NPS would be funded in a way that is flexible, multi-year, and stable, allows both operational and capital spending, and increases with demand. The existing model is the opposite of that ideal, as shown in Table 8.3.

Table 8.3 Funding model of NPS

Characteristic	Current funding model	Desirable funding model
Time frame	Annual	Multi-year, multi-generational
Stability	Volatile, unreliable	Stable, predictable
Uses of funds	Operations, inflexible	Operations and capital, flexible
Growth	Flat	Growing with increased demand on the NPS

Towards a sustainable funding model

The fundamental flaw in the current funding model is that the mission of the NPS – to keep these places 'unimpaired' and useable by the public *forever* – is incompatible with its stream of revenues. 'Perpetuity' missions require sources of funding that are stable, flexible and aligned with a long-term time horizon. By contrast, NPS funding is volatile and short-term. Not only are appropriations uncertain, but fee income fluctuates (according to the number of visitors and events) and the annual payout from the LWCF is unpredictable. The level of philanthropic contributions also varies according to economic and other exogenous factors. Consequently, the underlying financial base of the institution of the NPS is inadequate to maintain the existing assets and infrastructure in a state of good repair.

Most institutions with long-term perpetuity missions, including universities, hospitals, museums, churches, performing arts groups (such as symphonies and choirs), and charities rely on sources of funding that are structured to be sustainable over the long term, such as endowments, bond issuance, and multi-year budget cycles. Each of these techniques should be explored for the NPS.

The proposals outlined should be viewed as the beginning of a wider discussion on how to protect the NPS, including its places, monuments, landscapes, and programs, for the next generation. They should be viewed as complementary to overall improvement in the Federal funding for land-based agencies, such as fully funding the LWCF and allowing for more oil and gas drilling revenues to be directed to the Department of Interior.

Establishing an NPS endowment for long-term sustainability

The explicit purpose of an endowment is to link past, current, and future generations. It allows an institution to make commitments far into the future, knowing that resources to meet those commitments will continue to be available to support the mission of the institution in perpetuity.

Endowments can *supplement*—not replace—annual funding from appropriations, fees, and other sources. The idea of an endowment is that aggregated donations today can be invested to deliver a long-term stable return that becomes a second source of funding that may be specified for particular purposes. In the case of the NPS, where Federal funding is disproportionately budgeted for operations within each Park, an endowment could provide a sustainable source of income to pay for investing in maintenance, repair, land acquisition and system-wide programming that is chronically underfunded by Congress. Endowment funds may be invested conservatively in U.S. treasuries and managed by the NPF (the legally constituted philanthropic arm of the NPS).

An endowment could grow to produce a substantial amount of revenue. The bipartisan Second Century Commission called for the establishment of an NPS endowment in its final report in [insert year]. Since 2016, Congress has been considering a proposal that would set up an endowment-like entity called the 'National Park Service Legacy Restoration Fund'. The fund would be paid for by a portion of oil and gas revenues and be dedicated to eradicating the NPS maintenance backlog and related efforts. This model would be straightforward for the current governance structure.

However, there are other sources of funding that could be used to fund or contribute to an endowment. These could include a one-time congressional appropriation to launch the fund, perhaps in conjunction with a national capital matching campaign.

More directly, the NPS should be permitted to divert some portion of unspent annual visitor fees to the endowment, given that the public pays such fees for the explicit purpose of supporting the Park unit. In addition, NPS should be given the right to invest the interest accrued on visitor and camping fees into an endowment. These fees and interest would therefore constitute a way for today's NPS visitors to contribute to the long-term viability of NPS.

There are many models for administering an endowment. For example, Gallaudet University for the Deaf is a quasi-governmental entity that gives flexibility to administrators but regulates the usage of funds for ethical and legal purposes. The Smithsonian, although smaller than NPS, operates through a combination of Federal appropriations and its own private trust fund assets. These include contributions from private sources (endowments; donations from individuals, corporations, and foundations; and memberships) and revenues from the Smithsonian Enterprises operation (magazines, mail-order catalog, product development, entertainment, shops, restaurants, and concessions). One of the main benefits that Smithsonian derives from its funding structure is that it has greater flexibility in spending money. For example, it can hire staff (such as art experts and historians) outside the federal employment structure and use a combination of private and public funds to make acquisitions.

However constituted, an endowment fund could provide several direct benefits to the NPS, including greater stability, flexibility and the ability to plan investments over a longer time horizon. Having greater certainty over its long-term capital investment plan would also enable the NPS to leverage its other sources of revenue, especially local philanthropic donations, by working with local partners to raise funds. Depending on the purposes that were authorized for the fund, an NPS endowment could enable the NPS to attain higher levels of quality than would otherwise be possible, for example by investing in new technologies and physical assets that would help to achieve the mission over the longer-term.

Allowing the NPS to issue bonds

A basic premise of finance is that financing mechanisms should match the life of the asset. So for example, a city may issue a 20-year bond to finance a new tunnel, ensuring that the cost is distributed fairly among those who will use the tunnel during its lifespan. The use of bonds to finance projects is warranted when the initial outlay is large and the project itself will produce benefits that will be enjoyed over a long period.

The NPS maintains numerous long-term assets, including both NPS holdings themselves (such as historical sites) as well as infrastructure to support public access and maintenance. Accordingly, it would be appropriate for the NPS to issue bonds in certain situations, as outlined above.

The idea of allowing the NPS to issue debt has been discussed for decades. Annson (1999) pointed out that many of the National Parks' critical capital funding requirements (such as transportation systems and sewage repairs) could be met through the issuance of bonds, as well as potentially transformative long-term investments in scientific research and development of new education/interpretive programs. The interest on these bonds could be serviced through visitor fees, which are not dependent on congressional appropriations.

Issuing bonds does not 'create' more revenue, but it provides a mechanism for the NPS to 'move money across time' – that is, to amortize the cost over the lifecycle of the asset (Lee et al., 1998). This makes sense for the NPS, which can reasonably expect that generations of visitors will enjoy the investment. A Harvard paper that examined this concept in 1998 pointed out that bonds are not free (interest must be paid to bondholders, and tax-exempt bonds are subsidized to some extent by the general taxpayer). However, the authors agreed that issuing bonds in some cases would give the NPS a flow of long-term financing and should be considered as part of a package of reforms to enhance the agency's financial base.

A slightly different approach would be to give the NPS authority to join local governments in issuing bonds. Local jurisdictions with good bond ratings have access to the $3.8 trillion-dollar municipal bond market. For example, gateway communities that surround the National Parks may levy bonds in partnership with NPS units to help fund the construction of alternative transportation systems. Such joint bonding authority would provide Park officials with the potential to meet critical needs in their respective NPS units in an economically feasible way. Another option would be to allow individual NPS units to issue bonds that are guaranteed by local adjacent communities, enabling the NPS units to borrow at favorable municipal bond rates.

The creation of NPS bonds or NPS-linked bonds would feed into the growing investor appetite for 'Green Bonds'. While most investors still view green bonds as a niche product in the overall fixed income market, green bonds have grown rapidly to nearly $74.6 billion in issuance in 2018 – more than double the volume of $37 billion in 2014[5]. During 2018 there were 670 green bond issues, including 491 from the USA, 36 from Sweden, and 35 from China. Although this market is not yet mature, the demand for secure green assets may prove very attractive, especially for the least glamorous of projects such as water and sewer improvements, which have proved to be a 'sweet spot' for local governments experimenting with green bond issues.

If structured correctly, allowing NPS Parks to issue debt would establish a mechanism for all Americans to invest in the NPS units, indirectly. It may also be possible for small-denomination 'mini-bonds' (used in some cities and local jurisdictions) that allow individuals to purchase small denominations starting as low as $500[6]. Our survey of economic value demonstrates that there is significant 'passive-use value', in which those who seldom visit the NPS units nevertheless place a high value on them. This value could be captured if the public had a low-risk opportunity (through general fund investing) to participate in funding the long-term sustainability of the NPS units.

Providing the NPS with two-year Federal appropriations

One way to reduce volatility in the congressional appropriations cycle is simply to do it less frequently. Biennial appropriations are used in a number of states and local governments and have been adopted by the U.S. Department of Veterans Affairs (VA), in an effort to mitigate against the disruptions of short-term congressional budgeting. This approach also makes sense for the NPS.

The arguments for biennial appropriations are that they smooth the appropriations process and make it easier for agencies to award long-term (usually less expensive) contracts, to enter into longer-term partnerships with state, local, and private partners, and assist the planning process. From the congressional perspective, biennial bills give lawmakers more time to spend on oversight of agencies, instead of tinkering with small adjustments to budgets that are largely incremental. When the VA was given a two-year appropriation in 2012, this reform was intended to make it easier for the VA to rebuild its fixed assets, such as hospital infrastructure, and to ensure that services to veterans were not disrupted.

Although many government agencies would like to enjoy the security of two-year budget cycles, NPS is one of the best candidates. Like the VA, NPS enjoys strong bipartisan support. But it has suffered disproportionately from the widespread dysfunction in federal budgeting that has led to 22 government shutdowns (and dozens of threatened shutdowns) since 1974. As a 'non-essential agency' the NPS has to plan for contingencies of how to handle an 'orderly shutdown' of 419 places. This causes extra expense and problems not only for the NPS, but for its partners in state and local government, private contractor concessions, and local communities dependent on visitors to the National Parks.

Moreover, NPS is largely seasonal, with 48 percent of its visitors arriving between the months of June and September[7]. Even without a shutdown, the uncertainty of when Congress will enact its annual appropriations bill for the agency leaves NPS without a predictable source of funding. This creates significant problems for an 'operational' agency such as the NPS. During a short-term continuing resolution (CR), the Park budget is allocated on a pro-rata basis, (e.g. if the CR is only for three months, then the Park gets only 25% of its budget with no guarantee the residual will come). Projects get delayed and hiring for the summer is stalled, forcing a scramble just before summer to get ready when the budget finally comes.

The NPS can further point out that its income from fees, LWCF funding, and other sources are highly volatile and that it needs to have stability for appropriated funds. Finally, the amount of appropriations to the NPS has been stable for the past 20 years and growing at a very slow incremental pace. In this instance, the lack of increase in NPS appropriations is an argument that it should at least have the predictability of two years of funding, which would enable NPS to better plan for contracts, raise philanthropic dollars, and set up longer-term strategic alliances.

Reforming the NPS's commercial relationships (user/entrance fees and concessions)

Entrance fee revenues

Reforming the fee structure could provide a stable and more flexible source of funding, if revised by legislation. A revised fee statute must clarify that that fees cannot serve as a 'replacement' for annual appropriations, but rather they must be used to address maintenance backlog, resource and visitor enhancements. Moreover, fees should not be permitted to be collected or used as a substitute for government funding in the event of a shutdown.

Second, the new system should be changed to allow more flexible use of the fees. This includes changing the 80/20 allocation between fee-based NPS units and non-fee NPS units to 50/50, and granting the NPS Director the authority to plan and execute new special-use fees (such as backcountry camping) where appropriate and with public input.

Third, the fees could be leveraged to enable the NPS to earn more revenues. The fees themselves should be placed in a Federal Treasury interest-bearing account with the annual interest accrued transferred to the NPF endowment, as described previously. Additionally, the NPS should be permitted to use the revenue stream from fees to service infrastructure bonds.

Finally, the NPS should be given the authority to enter into revenue-sharing agreements with commercial entities who use the Parks, such as filming permittees.

Concessions

The right to operate concessions in popular U.S. NPS units must be viewed from a different perspective. These concessions benefit directly from the taxpayer dollars and fees that support the NPS units, and in many cases enjoy a near-monopoly on iconic views and locations, as well as a guaranteed stream of visitors. It is a privilege for private companies to operate these concessions. The system must be further modified to maximize the income that the NPS derives from this partnership with the private sector, as well as to enable the NPS to be a full partner in renovations and maintenance.

A key reform that would generate new revenue for the NPS is to create an 'enterprise' arm of the NPF that would build, upgrade and operate the commercial services within the National Parks. This would replace the current concessions program where private sector businesses operate food, beverage, lodging, transportation and guide services within NPS units while paying a small franchise fee to the NPS. Under the current model, the profits from these operations are kept by the private companies as return to their owners or shareholders. Under a new 'enterprise' model, these profits would be returned to the NPS through the NPF, providing benefit directly to the Park visitor, who is the ultimate shareholder of the National Parks. This new enterprise function would have the authority, with approval of the NPS, to explore new commercial operations, long term leases, and fee-for-service contracts.

Providing flexibility in how philanthropic dollars can be used by the NPS

Greater flexibility in accepting and using philanthropic gifts would be beneficial to allow the NPS to better fulfill its mission. Under current appropriations law, federal funds cannot be 'co-mingled' with philanthropic funds for project execution. Donated funds can be transferred to the Federal government for a project, but those funds are then treated as if they were appropriated and subject to all the Federal rules. Federal funds cannot be transferred to a partner organization to execute a project within an NPS unit. When contemplating a project that is jointly funded, this situation requires a convoluted workaround, awkwardly splitting projects into distinct parts (e.g., the parking lot vs. the new visitor center building) with the NPS paying for one contract and the partner paying for the other. This can result in two contracts, which increases the overall cost.

New 'partnership' authority is needed to allow more flexibility on project execution when the Federal government is only providing a portion of the funding and the balance is being provided by philanthropy. The Smithsonian Institution already has a more flexible model, that allows the parts of Smithsonian to have greater flexibility in hiring and acquiring exhibits when there is funding from both government and private sources. The NPS would benefit from a new partnership authority and less cumbersome process of revenue sharing. Greater flexibility in this area is likely to encourage philanthropists and the general public to give more generously to the NPS, and to donate to a wider range of needs.

Conclusion

The NPS and its mission—to preserve these places 'unimpaired' for public use and recreation—enjoys extraordinary public support. Beloved though they are, the Parks face multiple threats to their survival, such as climate change, growing tourism, decaying infrastructure, and declining federal financial support. The current level of funding barely covers the basic operating costs of the agency, with more of the infrastructure falling into disrepair every year. Even if Congress awards the agency a one-time infusion of money to address the maintenance backlog, it will not be sufficient to maintain and replenish the assets over the next century.

The parks need a new financial model that is better aligned with their mission. In this chapter, we have proposed a series of reforms that would provide the NPS with a more long-term, stable, and sustainable source of operating revenues and capital. These include (a) establishing an endowment; (b) allowing the NPS to issue bonds to fund infrastructure investments; (c) adopting biennial appropriations; (d) reforming the fee and concession structure and granting more flexibilities to the NPS director; and (e) expanding the role and definition of philanthropy and partnerships. These changes need to be accompanied by an overall national commitment to protecting public lands and distinctive places, for example, by funding the LWCF and directing greater amounts of oil and gas revenues to conservation and preservation activities. Together, such reforms could help protect America's best investment for future generations.

Notes

1 The total number of acres in the NPS has increased by only 0.8%, due to the small size of most of these new units (Comway, 2018).
2 The Highway Trust Fund finances most federal government spending for highways and mass transit. Revenues for the trust fund come from transportation-related excise taxes, primarily federal taxes on gasoline and diesel fuel.
3 When automobiles were first allowed into national parks in 1908, fees were levied to pay for road improvements.
4 Examples of 'rustic park architecture' include the Many Glacier Hotel in Glacier National Park, the El Tovar in Grand Canyon National Park and the Old Faithful Inn in Yellowstone National Park. These were government owned facilities, operated by the private sector under a contract.
5 https://www.climatebonds.net/files/files/H1%202018%20Highlights_120720 18.pdf
6 See https://neighborly.com/
7 NPS IRMA Statistics https://irma.nps.gov/Stats/Reports/National

References

Annson, R. 1999. Funding our National Parks in the 21st century: will we be able to preserve and protect our embattled National Parks? *Fordham Environmental Law Review* 11: 1–58.

Comay, L. 2018. *National Park Service Appropriations: Ten-Year Trends.* Congressional Research Service, Washington, DC. July 10.

Congressional Budget Office. 2018. *The Budget and Economic Outlook: 2018 to 2028.* Congressional Budget Office, Washington, DC.

duPont, C.M., J. Levitt, and L. Bilmes. 2016. Green bonds and land conservation: a new investment landscape? *Stanford Social Innovation Review* December 2016.

Lee, H., H. Leonard, J. Walder, P. Zimmerman, and W. Vanasselt. 1998. National Park Bonds: A Patch or a Panacea. Environment and Natural Resources Program, Belfer Center for Science and International affairs, and Center for Business and Government, John F. Kennedy School of Government, Harvard University, Cambridge, MA.

Potrero Group. 2016. National Park Partners, Status and Trends. http://potrerog roup.com/files/pdfs/PotreroGroup_NPF_Status-and-Trends.pdf.

U.S. Department of Interior. 2017. NPS Overview. Washington, DC, January.

Vincent, C.H. 2018. *Land and Water Conservation Fund: Overview, Funding History, and Issues.* Congressional Research Service, Washington, DC, 17 August 2018.

White House Budget Authority. 2019. https://www.whitehouse.gov/wp-content/up loads/2018/02/budauth-fy2019.xlsx.

9 Conclusion
Benefits of National Parks extend far beyond visitation and tourism

John B. Loomis and Linda J. Bilmes

Introduction

This book is the first comprehensive effort to quantify the economic benefits of the U.S. National Parks. Using our conservative methodology, the benefits add up to about $100 billion annually, of which more than one-third accrues to people who never set foot in the National Park Service units (NPS units) themselves. While visitation and associated tourism are the most visible benefits to the public, these are just one of the many values provided by the National Parks and other protected areas. The full range of values include:

- Existence and bequest benefits from knowing the areas are protected today and for future generations, respectively.
- Benefits from the educational materials about history, culture, and nature.
- Benefits from mitigating the impact of climate change through storing carbon.
- Benefits from the iconic images and scenery from the National Parks and protected areas used in movies and television programs.

Many park agencies generate additional benefits through their work with state and local stakeholders to help protect areas of natural, historical, and cultural significance specific to their local communities. In the National Park Service (NPS) this function is known as cooperative programming.

Most of our research is based on new data collected specifically to quantify the many values of NPS units. While we have not always been able to quantify every benefit, in Chapter 2 we have demonstrated and applied a method for estimating the dollar value the American public holds for NPS units and programs. The magnitude of these estimated benefits is striking:

- $62 billion is the total economic value to the American public of NPS units. Roughly half of this relates to recreation usage; the other half is for non-use values such as existence value (knowing the NPS units exist) and bequest value (knowing the NPS units are preserved for future generations);

- $30 billion is the value to the American public of NPS cooperative programming that aids communities in protecting historical, cultural and natural resources as well as in providing educational services to school-age children.

Chapter 3 presents the methods, data, and results of the NPS's analysis of tourism-related economic contributions from the 300 million visitors to NPS units:

- Economic contribution of $36 billion to the national economy.
- Supporting over 300,000 jobs.

Chapter 4 presents a method to quantify and value the amount of carbon stored in NPS units. Our results indicated that:

- Nearly $1 billion in value is created from NPS in the Lower 48 states units storing (sequestering) vegetative carbon so as to limit the impact of emissions on climate.

In Chapter 5, we present a detailed valuation of specific types of educational materials developed by the NPS, and of the opportunities provided for experiential learning to both children and adults. In this chapter we analyze the Golden Gate National Recreation Area, where the NPS developed teacher materials and other NPS web-based learning material. We conclude that:

- About $1 billion in direct national benefits are provided by the NPS in the form of educational benefits.

Chapter 6 categorizes NPS units in terms of how they are utilized in movies and TV programs. The categories are:

- 'Iconic places' that are used to establish the location of a critical scene (e.g., Statue of Liberty with New York City).
- 'Grand natural places' that allow movie and TV producers to 'transport' the viewer to another time period (e.g., the western frontier before development) or to another planet (e.g. *Star Wars*).
- Undeveloped natural landscape that is located within 30 miles of Hollywood studios (e.g., Santa Monica Mountains National Recreation Area).

A complete count of all movies and TV shows filmed in NPS units is difficult since the NPS does not have a centralized system for tracking filming permits. However, our research documented:

- More than 30 blockbuster movies with one or more scenes shot in NPS units.

- Over 20 well-known movies or TV shows filmed in and around the NPS Santa Monica Mountains National Recreation Area alone.

The NPS currently collects an extremely small fee relative to the movies' gross revenues for access to the Parks. We present a method for inferring the contribution of the NPS unit to these gross revenues and apply this to one movie to illustrate the data required and data sources and calculations involved.

Chapter 7 discusses how NPS partners with a wide variety of stakeholders outside of NPS units to assist them in accomplishing:

- Preservation of historic structures of local importance outside of NPS units.
- Transfer of other Federal lands to be used as local recreation areas.

The NPS does this through:

- Providing technical expertise in design, developing materials and training to stakeholders.
- Cost sharing on projects.

This kind of cooperative programming with state and local agencies as well as non-governmental organizations creates added visibility for the NPS and its mission to people who may not visit NPS units themselves.

Implications of the Benefit estimates for funding

We titled this book *Valuing National Parks: America's Best Investment* because, even using conservative estimates, about $100 billion in benefits to the American public are generated by the NPS units and cooperative programming each year using a budget of just $2.5 billion. The inadequacy of this budget is evident in the backlog of $12 billion in deferred maintenance and restoration projects due to a lack of funding. The backlog includes infrastructure such as recreation facilities, roads, bridges, water, and sewers to accommodate the 300 million-plus visitors each year. It also includes repairs to historical monuments to maintain their historical value, reducing forest fuels to prevent forest fires, controlling invasive species, etc. The very high rate of return provided by the NPS on its budget implies that funding this deferred maintenance would more than likely be a sound investment.

Attempting to eliminate this backlog solely through visitor fees is inappropriate for two reasons. First, many of the NPS units are already used to capacity and cannot accommodate more use[1]. Second, attempting to increase the NPS budget by simply raising entrance fees does not meet the 'benefits received' equity principle of public finance—that groups of individuals should pay for government programs in relation to the benefits they receive (Tresch, 1981; Starett, 1991: 104). As the preceding chapters have documented, the NPS provides many benefits to non-visitors through educational materials developed for teachers, carbon sequestration, and cooperative programming with stakeholders outside of NPS units.

In Chapter 8 we outline various funding options that range from small operational changes to major structural changes in how the NPS is funded to match its dual mandate. These options are not mutually exclusive. To protect the National Park assets that generate the large public benefits documented in this book, some combination will be required to put the NPS's finances on a more sustainable footing. Thus, our recommendations provide a legislative agenda that could be incorporated in part or in whole in future legislation.

The funding options we identify are as follows:

- Establish an NPS endowment fund using donations to the National Park Foundation (NPF). The long-term stable annual returns from the investments in this endowment could supplement annual congressional appropriations. The Smithsonian Institution[2] operates in this manner.
- Allow the NPS to issue bonds. Such bonds could be used to finance large capital projects that exceed what can be funded with a single fiscal year appropriation. The bonds could be repaid from entrance fees and other NPS revenue streams.
- Provide the NPS with a two-year Federal appropriation. This would reduce the volatility in the congressional appropriations cycle. A similar reform was implemented for the U.S. Department of Veteran Affairs to reduce disruptions in the provision of services to veterans.
- Reform the Federal Land Recreation Enhancement Act that governs fee collection. This would provide the NPS (and other Federal agencies) greater flexibility in the use of such funds, including backing the issuance of NPS bonds.
- Reform the structure of NPS concessionaire contracts, potentially replacing concessions with an 'enterprise' within the NPF. With this structure, revenue in excess of costs could be returned to the NPS.
- Provide flexibility in how philanthropic gifts can be used by NPS. Currently, funds from such gifts cannot be directly combined with federal appropriations. Consequently, the NPS sometimes has difficulty generating a sufficiently large sum of money to fund major capital projects, the cost of which often exceeds either a gift or appropriations alone.

Conclusion

This book provides the first comprehensive framework for valuing National Parks and other protected areas, whether wilderness, wildlife refuges, state parks, or regional parks. We have focused on the U.S. National Parks, but these methods can be a starting point for economists and park professionals the world over to quantify the many values provided by their own parks and protected areas.

We hope the insights provided in the book provide some motivation for collecting additional data and for better record-keeping of data that is collected. Analysts cannot value what field offices do not count.

In other cases, the relevant data exists but needs to be purchased and analyzed. For example, analysis of existing house sales data has been done to measure the gain in residential property values adjacent to protected natural areas. Examples include the gain in residential property values near wildlife refuges (Taylor et al., 2012; Neumann et al., 2009), wilderness areas (Phillips, 2000), and local parks (Crompton, 2001). This has not been done for U.S. National Parks.

Some of the difficulty in measuring economic values provided to society from parks and other protected areas is due to a lack of long-term monitoring of the benefits people receive. To start addressing this limitation, NPS social scientists have begun a program of socioeconomic monitoring of visitors to NPS units. The U.S. Forest Service National Visitor Use Monitoring program provides information on visitor satisfaction and perceived benefits. This program, which began in 2000, samples each National Forest every five years. Both of these programs illustrate the systematic and comprehensive efforts needed to derive accurate estimates of long-term visitor benefits. A parallel set of surveys is also needed to regularly measure the non-use or passive-use value to non-visitors.

As technology evolves, new types of 'uses' of Parks, protected areas, and their wildlife will emerge. For example, remote webcams allow non-visitors to 'virtually' enjoy the scenery and wildlife of remote Parks and protected areas[3]. At this point, it is not clear whether virtual reality will be a substitute or a complement to physical visits. As the richness of virtual reality improves, it may open the opportunity to those who cannot travel to these parks or protected areas to at least glimpse of what a visitor might see. It is important for agencies to count such virtual visitors when calculating the full benefits that their protected areas provide (see Loomis et al., 2018 for an NPS example).

We believe this book documents the large economic value of the National Parks to the American public. The book should serve as inspiration for park staff, managers, economists, and analysts to build on these methods to help preserve natural, historical, and cultural resources for our generation and for those generations to come. We also hope policymakers can take the information in this book to provide the NPS with the support the agency needs to make the agency's second century as successful as its first.

Notes

1 See Church (2015).
2 The Smithsonian is a collection of 19 museums and nine research centers.
3 Loomis et al. (2018) provide a methodology and example for brown bear viewing in Katmai National Park in Alaska.

References

Church, Lisa J. 2015. Heavy traffic forces shutdown at entrance to Arches N.P. *The Times-Independent.* https://moabtimes.com/2015/05/28/26659449-heavy-traffic-forces-shutdown-at-entrance-to-arches-n-p/

Crompton, J. 2001. The impact of parks on property values: a review of the empirical evidence. *Journal of Leisure Research* 33(1): 1–31.

Loomis, J., L. Richardson, C. Huber, J. Skibins, and R. Sharp. 2018. A method to value nature-related webcam viewing: the value of virtual use with application to brown bear webcam viewing. *Journal of Environmental Economics and Policy* 7(4): 452–462.

Neumann, B., K. Boyle, and K. Bell. 2009. Property price effects of a national wildlife refuge. *Land Use Policy* 26(4): 1011–1019.

Phillips, S. 2000. Windfalls for wilderness: Land protection and land value in the Green Mountains, pp. 258–267. In *Wilderness Science in a Time of Change Conference*, vol. 2. S. F. McCool, D. N. Cole, W. T. Borrie, and J. O'Loughlin. (Eds.). USDA For. Serv., Rocky Mountain Research Station, Ogden, UT.

Starrett, D. 1988. *Foundations of Public Economics.* Cambridge, UK: Cambridge University Press.

Taylor, L., X. Liu, and T. Hamilton. 2012. Amenity Values of Proximity to National Wildlife Refuges. https://www.fws.gov/economics/ecosystemServices/Amenity%20Value%20of%20Proximity%20to%20NWR.pdf.

Tresch, R. 1981. *Public Finance.* Plano, TX: Business Publications Inc.

Index

Italic page numbers indicate figures while **bold** page numbers mark tables.

Printed in the United States
by Baker & Taylor Publisher Services

Printed in the United States
by Baker & Taylor Publisher Services